THE BATTLE
OF CLONMULT

The IRA's Worst Defeat

THE BATTLE OF CLONMULT

The IRA's Worst Defeat

3900800038087/
441·5/Red
PTC/07

Tom O'Neill

NONSUCH

First published 2006

Nonsuch Publishing Limited
73 Lower Leeson Street
Dublin 2
Ireland
www.nonsuchireland.com

National Library Cataloguing in Publication Data.
A catalogue record for this book is available from the National Library.

ISBN 1 84588 554 6

Typesetting and origination by Tempus Publishing Limited
Printed and bound in Great Britain

Contents

Acknowledgements

The research and completion of this book would not have been possible without the co-operation, assistance and support of a number of individuals. I was extremely fortunate to have Mr. Gabriel Doherty as my supervisor in University College Cork, for my M.A. thesis in Local History, for which 'The Battle of Clonmult' was my chosen subject. I want to thank him for his guidance, advice and encouragement. To Mai Kerins must go special thanks for her assistance and support throughout. She was of immense assistance to me right from the start and she did invaluable work in proofreading this text with her friend, Miss Sandra McKeown. They both read this book from cover to cover and left few pages unimproved.

I wish to thank the Officer Commanding, Irish Military Archives, Cathal Brugha Barracks, Dublin, Comdt. Victor Laing and his staff, for their efficiency in producing copies of the Bureau of Military History, Witness Statements. Thanks also to Mr. Jonathan Armstrong, head librarian, and Miss Ciara McGettigan, assistant librarian, of the Honourable Society of King's Inns, Dublin, to the staff of the Local Studies section of the Cork city Library, to Mr. Michael Lynch and Miss Patti-Ann O'Leary, of the Local Studies section of the Kerry County Library, Tralee. I wish to thank the staff of the reference department of the National Library of Ireland, Dublin and in particular Mr. Tom Desmond. Thanks also to the staff of the Cork Archive Institute, and the Special Collections Dept., (Q–1), U.C.C., to Miss Amanda Moreno of the Royal Irish Fusiliers Museum, Armagh, to the archivist of the Royal Hampshire Regiment Museum, and to Mr. Tony Richards of the Imperial War Museum, London. In east Cork I am grateful to the following for supplying information: Miss Mary Murnane, daughter of Volunteer Mick Murnane, Miss Eimer Burke, daughter of Capt. Michael Burke and niece of Capt. James Ahern. Thanks to Miss Ursula O'Mahony, Mr. John McAuliffe, Mr. Pete Morrisson, Mr. David Desmond, nephew of the two Desmond brothers, Mr. John Joe Joyce, nephew of Volunteer John Joe Joyce and Mr. M. O'Connor, nephew of Volunteer Christopher O'Sullivan. I am also indebted to Mr. John Mulcahy of Whitechurch, County Cork, for locating the British Army reports of the battle; these have been misfiled at the P.R.O. at Kew.

It was a privilege to interview Mr. Jim Hegarty, a native of Clonmult and a witness to the battle, and his wife Josephine. Many thanks to Miss Pauline Cotter for arranging the interviews, also to her mother Mrs. Theresa Cotter herself a noted historian, for all her assistance. To Mr. Tomás O Riordán for providing some valuable information. To my brother Vincent, for his involvement in the Battle of Clonmult lectures. To the O'Sullivan family, the present owners of the battle site at Garrylaurence, Clonmult, for permission to visit the site.

I would also like to thank the following for giving me permission to use the photographs featured in this book: Mrs. C. Walsh Ballyspillane, Midleton, Mr. John P. McAuliffe, Midleton, Mr John Joe Joyce, Midleton, Cork Archives Institute, The Kerryman Newspaper via National Library, Dublin, The Imperial War Museum London, John Harty, Cloyne, Co. Cork.

All of these individuals have helped me in the course of my research into this work. Any errors or omissions are entirely my own.

I hope that anyone whose copyright my book has unwittingly infringed will accept my sincere apology.

This book is dedicated to my wife Ann and our sons Finbarr and Philip. Thanks for the support and patience.

List of Abbreviations

A. S. U.	Active Service Unit
C.B.	Companion of the Order of the Bath
C.C.	Catholic Curate
C.O.	Commanding Officer
Col.	Colonel
Comdt.	Commandant (Irish equivalent of a British Army major)
C.I.	County Inspector (R.I.C)
C.S.M.	Company Sergeant Major
D.I.	District Inspector (R.I.C)
Div.	Division
D.S.O.	Distinguished Service Order
Gen.	General
G.H.Q.	General Headquarters
I.G.	Inspector General (R.I.C)
I.O.	Intelligence Officer
I.R.A.	Irish Republican Army
Lt.	Lieutenant (Irish)
Liut.	Lieutenant (British Army)
Lt. Col.	Lieutenant-Colonel
M.B.E.	Member of the Order of the British Empire
M.C.	Military Cross (bravery medal)
M.M.	Military Medal (bravery medal)
O.C.	Officer Commanding (of a company)
Q.M. Officer	Quartermaster Officer
T.C.I.	Temporary County Inspector (R.I.C)
Vol.	Volunteer

CHAPTER 1

The lead up to the Battle of Clonmult, 1913–1920

In this chapter I want to briefly cover in chronological order the political and military events, both national and local, from 1913 to December 1920, which led to the Battle of Clonmult. I also want to introduce the individuals who were involved in the Flying Column of the 4th Battalion, First Cork Brigade I.R.A., the unit involved at Clonmult. It was the men from these columns, using a combination of the appropriate strategies and a political mandate based on the support of the people, who made the War of Independence possible.

The public meeting which inaugurated the Irish Volunteers in Cork city and county was held in the old City Hall at 8.30 p.m. on the evening of Sunday, 14th of December, 1913.[1] The principal speakers were Eoin Mc Neill and Sir Roger Casement; also in attendance was Tomás MacCurtain, the future Lord Mayor of Cork and officer commanding the First Cork Brigade. During the first six months of 1914, a Volunteer Company was set up in Cobh which was one of the first in what was to become the 4th Battalion area.[2] Jack O'Connell was originally a member of Redmond's Volunteers but after the split of September 1914, he joined the Irish Volunteers in March, 1915.[3] Other men from Cobh who were active in the Volunteer movement from this period, were Paddy Whelan, Daithi O'Brien, O.C., 'A' (Cobh) Company during the 'Tan War', Michael Leahy who became C.O. of the 4th Battalion and James Ahern.[4]

The Volunteers were mobilised at Sheares Street in Cork city during Easter week of 1916. Their mission was to act as security for the distribution of the arms and ammunition that was expected from the gun-running ship *Aud*. However, as a result of the capture and scuttling of the vessel, the men returned to the city empty handed. On account of conflicting orders from Dublin and a lack of direct communications with their superiors in Dublin, the Cork Units did not play an active role during Easter Week.

In the immediate post 1916 Rising period, the British authorities made at least two major errors. Firstly, they executed the leaders and overnight turned these men into martyrs. Secondly, they interned 1,863 of the insurgents in a disused distillery in Frongoch, North Wales.[5] This internment camp has been aptly described as 'a university of revolution'.[6] This in my opinion, was the greater error because it brought together many of the leading individuals of the War of Independence: Michael Brennan of Clare, Michael Collins, Tomás MacCurtain and Terence McSweeney of Cork, Mick Leahy of Cobh,[7] Tom McEllistrim of Kerry, Dick McKee, Dick Mulcahy and Sean T. O'Kelly of Dublin, to name but a few.

It was at Frongoch that the lessons of the Rising were debated and the strategies and tactics of the 'Tan War' were planned. It was decided that they would never again take on the might of the Crown Forces using conventional warfare.[8] The next war would utilise guerrilla warfare; no more taking over buildings and waiting to be attacked. It was at Frongoch that it was recognised that priority must be given to destroying the Royal Irish Constabulary and the 'G' Division of the Dublin Metropolitan Police, who between them were seen as the eyes and ears of Dublin Castle, monitoring every corner of Ireland. Also, the network of contacts that were essential to conducting a national resistance movement were forged during this long period of internment in north Wales. This camaraderie was the driving force behind the Irish Republican Army during the War of Independence, 1917–1921, a period described by the volunteers as the four glorious years.[9]

An Irish Volunteer Company was formed in Midleton towards the end of 1916. Jack O'Shea, John Brady and Sean Buckley were the Company officers.[10] Towards the end of 1917 the 4th Battalion companies were re-designated and Cobh became 'A' Company and Midleton became 'B' Company.

Paddy Higgins was the first company captain in the Aghada Company and remained in that appointment until late 1918 when he was re-appointed 4th Battalion Q.M. officer.[11] He joined the battalion Flying Column during December 1920. Joseph Aherne was active in the Volunteers in Midleton from the early days.[12] The parade ground was a walled enclosure in an old ruined castle yard at Cahermone, a short distance on the east side of the town. Their rifles were 'stout branches broken off nearby trees'.[13] Diarmuid O'Hurley, from Kilbrittan, west Cork, arrived in Midleton from Belfast in September 1918. He was soon after appointed O.C. of the Midleton Company.[14] Paddy Whelan, originally from Wexford, moved to Cobh where his father was employed by Irish Lights, and worked on the Daunt Rock lightship. Paddy began work as a boilermaker's apprentice in His Majesty's Dockyard, Haulbowline in September 1914.[15]

The activities covered in this book relate primarily to the Flying Column of the 4th Battalion, the First Cork Brigade and the Irish Republican Army. The territorial boundary of the battalion corresponded roughly with the old Parliamentary area of east Cork. The western boundary extended from Dunkettle Bridge north through Glanmire to Knockraha. The northern boundary was from Knockraha, east through Leamlara, Ballincurrig, Clonmult, Inch, Killeagh to Youghal. The southern boundary was the coastline from Youghal to Dunkettle including the Great Island.[16]

Up until 5th of January 1919, the First Cork Brigade covered all of county Cork.[17] On that date at a meeting held at Kilnadur, Dunmanway, which was chaired by Michael Collins who was representing G.H.Q., the county was divided into three brigades as it was proving almost impossible to administer.[18] The First Cork Brigade covered the city, west to Ballingeary and east to

Youghal, with Tomás MacCurtain in charge. The Second Brigade covered north Cork with Liam Lynch in charge, and the Third (West Cork) Brigade under Tom Hales, covered the western part of the county to the Kerry border.

There were ten battalions in the First Brigade and eighteen companies in the 4th Battalion. These Companies were located at Cobh, Midleton, Youghal, Knockgraha, Dungourney, Clonmult, Mogeely-Castlemarty, Lisgoold, Leamlara, Ladysbridge, Inch, Killeagh, Cloyne, Aghada, Shanagarry-Ballycotton, Ballymacoda, Churchtown South and Glounthaune; they carried the strength of over 1,000 men.[19] I have been unable to determine the designation of all of the companies but Cobh was 'A' Company, Midleton was 'B' and Knockgraha was 'E' Company. Youghal was later designated 10th Battalion.

One of the priorities of all active companies throughout the 'Tan War' was that of acquiring arms and ammunition. The I.R.A. obtained their weapons from a variety of sources. Initially, the Volunteers raided private houses and gun shops in their search for firearms, but this met with limited success, and the types of weapons procured generally only amounted to shotguns and .22" rifles which were quite useless against service .303" rifles.[20] Their main focus for weapons turned to the Crown Forces because service rifles, revolvers and ammunition were their primary requirement. The Irishmen who were home on leave from the British Army proved a fruitful source of service rifles. If the individual was lucky, he was offered money in exchange for the rifle but often there was no choice. The authorities soon cut off this source of weapons when armouries were made available in England to store the rifles of soldiers travelling home on leave to Ireland.

The General Election of December 1918 was a political turning point for Sinn Féin and the Republican movement. For these Nationalists it was a battle between the old Parliamentary Party and Sinn Féin. Of the 73 Republican candidates, 47 were in jail. The Sinn Féin election slogan was, 'Vote them in to get them out.' The election was a resounding victory for Sinn Féin. Of the

105 candidates returned for Ireland, 73 were Sinn Féin, 26 were Loyalist and just 6 were of the Parliamentary Party.[21] The elected Republicans refused to take their seats at Westminster and instead formed the First Dáil which met in the Mansion House in Dublin on the 21st of January 1919. The Dáil adopted three foundation deeds of which the 'Declaration of Independence' was of the greatest importance to the I.R.A.[22] This declared 'that a state of war existed which could never end until Ireland is definitely evacuated by the armed forces of England.'[23]

The Deputies standing, affirmed, 'we adopt this Declaration of Independence, and we pledge ourselves to put it into effect by every means in our power.'[24]

The I.R.A formed their principal means of power, and this 'Declaration of Independence' was seen by the I.R.A. as a mandate from the majority of the Irish people, through the Dáil, for a military campaign to be carried out against the British Forces. This formed the basis for their claim that they were the soldiers of the Irish Republic. In the eyes of those involved there was now an Irish political establishment with a military force ready for the impending war. The first shots of this war were heard in Soloheadbeg, Co. Tipperary the very same day as the First Dáil sat. Two R.I.C. constables, James McDonnell and Patrick O'Connell, were shot dead in an ambush by the men of the Third Tipperary Brigade.[25]

The men who were most active in the movement between 1918 and mid 1920, were part-time members. They worked at their civilian employment during the day, assembled for a raid or an attack during the night and returned to their work the following morning. Paddy Whelan, Jeremiah Aherne and Jack O'Connell, worked in the Midleton Engineering Works, prior to joining the column. Joseph Morrissey from Athlone, worked in Abernethy's Bakery in Castlemarty. Diarmuid O'Hurley worked as a foreman at T.S.R. Coppinger, Grain Merchants, 1 Main St., Midleton. It was here he received the nickname 'The Gaffer'. These early raids were quite successful as they generally had the element of surprise. The men involved at Clonmult were active in most of these operations.

Some of the early successes in east Cork included:

1. The capture and destruction of the Carrigtwohill R.I.C. Barracks, 3rd January 1920. The first such success in the country.
2. The capture of Castlemarty R.I.C. Barracks, 9th of February 1920.
3. British Army patrol disarmed near Cobh, one soldier killed.
4. Capture of Cloyne R.I.C. Barracks, 8th of May 1920.
5. Disarming of the joint Army/R.I.C. bicycle patrol at Mile Bush near Midleton, Saturday, 5th of June 1920. Twelve rifles captured.
6. British Army guard disarmed near Cobh, 25th of August 1920, one soldier killed. [26]
7. British mobile patrol attacked at Whiterock outside Midleton on the 26th of August, 1920, one soldier killed.

However, the authorities were building up intelligence on the activists and quite a few were arrested. The remainder, knowing they had been identified and were wanted, went 'on the run'. Tadhg Manley and Diarmuid O'Hurley were lodging at Mrs. Walsh's, 70 Chapel St., now St. Mary's Rd., in Midleton. A party of Cameron Highlanders raided the house on Monday, 7th of June 1920, two days after the Mile Bush ambush. Tadhg Manley was captured and O'Hurley only just managed to escape out the back door. [27] Tadhg Manley spent the remainder of the war in jail.

The introduction of the Restoration of Order in Ireland Act on August 9th, 1920, forced more men to go on the run. The authorities were finding it almost impossible to find jurors and this Act introduced internment without trial. It was a natural progression that those on the run, who were often living in the same safe houses, would eventually band together and this was the birth of the concept of the flying columns.

About this time, Ernie O'Malley,[28] Divisional Commander of the Second Southern Division, stated that, 'at the time and for sometime later, the men on the run were a bloody nuisance, for they lounged around, slept late, ate peoples food and did no work for the company or battalion in which they happened to be.'[29] However, the formation of the flying columns, which involved training and discipline, assimilated these men into an effective fighting force.

Towards the end of September 1920, the Flying Column of the 4th Battalion was formed at Knockgraha, approximately six kilometres east of the city, under the command of Diarmuid O'Hurley. Joseph Aherne, Jack Aherne, David and Michael Desmond, Michael Hallihan and Paddy Whelan were the first to report for duty with the column.[30] These men were the full-time members of the column from its formation until Clonmult. For a list of the other men known to have served in the column, see appendix 3, page 87.

The nature of the terrain around east Cork did not lend itself to the security of a large column. The terrain was too well served with roads and there were military garrisons at Cobh, Midleton, Youghal, Fermoy, Cork and Fort Carlisle near Whitegate. The average number serving on the column at any one time was generally limited to between sixteen and twenty. There were however, many men who were available at short notice to reinforce the column.[31] The rugged terrain of West Cork was much better suited to guerrilla warfare.

The General Headquarters of the I.R.A. recognised the benefit of the flying column and issued Operational Memos relating to them during September and October 1920.

Operational Order No. 1.

Devolved permission to carry out attacks on military and police patrols to officers of the rank of captain.

Operational Order No. 2

Ordered Brigade commandants to closely observe enemy formations so that no opportunity to attack them would be lost.

Operational Order No. 3

Ordered the interception of all police and military communications.

Operational Order No. 4

Ordered that the worst and most vicious of the R.I.C. were to be shot.

Operational Order No. 5.

Ordered that all Black and Tans were to be shot on sight.

Operational Order No. 6

Not found.

Operational Order No. 7

1. The flying column commander must endeavour to gain experience for himself and for his men by planning and then carrying out simple operations as outlined in Operational Orders No's 1 − 7.[32]
2. By harassing smaller and quieter military and police stations.
3. By intercepting and pillaging stores belonging to the enemy.
4. By intercepting communications.
5. By covering towns threatened by reprisal parties.

Following the stay at Knockraha, the column moved to Shanagarry in an attempt to engage the British, but without success. From here they travelled to Ballymacoda, Ladysbridge and on to Aghada, but again failed to make contact. They lay in ambush positions near Aghada on the 11th of December, expecting to engage a patrol from Fort Carlisle (Fort Davis), but again the British did not appear.[33] From Aghada, they marched to billet for the night in Bertie Walsh's house in Cloyne. This was a dangerous move as Walsh himself was on the run, and there was a possibility that the house was being watched. The house was surrounded by British troops the following morning and it was only through guile and an aggressive breakout that the column managed to escape.[34] The local Companies came rushing to their assistance after word reached them that the column was in difficulty. There were two similarities with Clonmult, in that there were no sentries in position and the house was surrounded. There was one major difference, the column members escaped from Cloyne but at Clonmult only one would escape.

The column moved from Cloyne to an unoccupied farmhouse at Kilmountain, about three miles east of Midleton, where they spent Christmas 1920. While there, word was received that a joint R.I.C./Black and Tan foot patrol operated on the Main Street of Midleton every night. The decision was taken by Diarmuid O'Hurley to attack the patrol on the night of the 29th of December. The entire column moved into Midleton under cover of darkness and the assembly area was at the sawmill on Charles Street. The twelve-man foot patrol left the R.I.C. Barracks at about 9.30 p.m. and proceeded down the Main Street. They were ambushed on the return leg of the patrol and in the fight, two Black and Tans, Ernest Dray and Arthur Thorp were killed.[35] During this operation, Vice-Commandant Joseph Aherne was in charge of a squad of volunteers that included Paddy Higgins and he was not impressed with Higgins's performance.[36] Joseph Aherne stated that Higgins on that occasion didn't show any great aptitude for the work'.[37] This observation was to have serious implications in the subsequent battle at Clonmult. A mobile patrol of police travelling from Cork in response to the attack, was itself ambushed at Ballyrichard near Carrigtwohill, and R.I.C. constable Martin Mullen was killed.[38] This mobile patrol was commanded by Temporary County Inspector (T.C.I.) J.J.T. Carroll, R.I.C.[39]

From Midleton, the column returned to their billet at Kilmountain and early in the New Year, moved to Griffins farmhouse at Cottstown, Dungourney.[40] From here they relocated to the disused farmhouse at Garrylaurence, on or around the 6th of January 1921, the scene of the Battle of Clonmult.

The Column's failed security plan

The men of the Flying Column had been in the disused farm-house at Garrylaurence, Clonmult for about five weeks. [41] The fact that they were there for so long infringed upon the normal activities of these I.R.A. formations and was in conflict with its title 'Flying,' which conjures up images of a type of commando, i.e. lightly armed, capable of hitting its enemy anywhere and constantly on the move.

To gain an insight into how such camps operated, one can refer to an account by Tom Barry, of a training camp for officers held in the Third (West Cork) Brigade area during the month September, 1920.[42] It was the norm for a training camp to last a minimum of seven days and to place a major emphasis on camp defence and security measures to avoid a surprise attack by British Forces.[43] A typical training program included lectures on engineering, first-aid and map reading.

The commander of any military formation is ultimately responsible for what is termed as 'terrain analyses'. Firstly, Commandant O'Hurley would have decided that the location of the training camp was suitable not only for the purpose of training but more importantly, the location had to be suitable from a security perspective. It had to be suitable for defence purposes and also to allow the opportunity to vacate the location while under fire should the situation arise. In the case of a guerrilla army, it was essential that the location be in an area where the local population were supportive of the cause.

In this instance, the location was certainly suitable for training as the terrain provided adequate facilities for conducting guerrilla style tactical training. The buildings provided suitable cover for the theory lessons essential for educating these part-time soldiers in the art of warfare. The buildings were large enough to billet approximately twenty members who would be present and the local population were very friendly.

It is generally accepted that no terrain will contain all of the essentials required for defence, so it is important that work be undertaken to improve and strengthen the defences. I have concluded that no such work was undertaken.

When carrying out terrain analysis, the commander should have examined the land around his position, in this case the farmhouse, not just from his inside vantage point but also from the view of an attacking force. The terrain surrounding the battle site today is quite different to what it was in 1921. Some of the ditches have been removed, but, more importantly, the wooded area north and north-west of the site extended much closer to the house. A map, surveyed in about 1904, clearly shows this.[44] The wooded area is important. On inspecting the 1904 Ordnance Survey map, it can be seen that the wood came within about two-hundred yards of the farmhouse. Forest paths can be seen on the map; they run in the direction from which the British troops approached and may well have been used by them as they provided a concealed ingress route.[45] The alleged informer, who had served in the British Army, would have been aware of the advantage afforded by these routes.

When the column occupied the farmhouse on or about the 6th of January 1921, emphasis was indeed placed on security. Two sentries were posted during the day and at night, two extra sentries were assigned to patrol the roads in the neighbourhood. All sentries were armed with a rifle, a revolver and a whistle with which to alert the other members in the event of danger. One of the sentries was also issued with a telescope during the day.[46] The nature of the terrain was such that the number of sentries was adequate provided they were properly briefed, remained alert and stayed at their posts.

Perimeter security, which was the responsibility of the sentries, was at times quite lax. Seamus Fitzgerald, T.D. in the First Dáil,

Chairman of the Parish Court, Cobh and President of East Cork District Court, visited the farmhouse about one week prior to the battle.

He related:

> I proceeded to Clonmult at once, and advanced towards the farmhouse in which the column was staying. I was, of course, guided safely after making the necessary contacts en route. I had expected to be challenged by their sentries, but I was in the farmhouse before I was recognised and brought inside to meet Paddy Whelan, Paddy Sullivan, Maurice Moore and young Glavin, all from Cobh, together with the other column men from Midleton and other units. [Diarmuid O'] Hurley was expected shortly, and when he arrived he challenged me crossly for having come. He must have been displeased with the easy manner in which I had approached without being properly challenged.[47]

The Column Commander, Commandant O'Hurley, when he analysed the surrounding terrain, looking for possible avenues of approach that the British Forces might use, would have seen five possible ingress routes. These were:

1. From Midleton via Dungourney and directly to Clonmult village.
2. From Dungourney using the Castlelyons road via Rathorgan cross roads.
3. From Fermoy through Castlelyons to Rathorgan cross roads.
4. From Tallow into Clonmult.
5. From Dungourney taking the upper road to Castlelyons and Fermoy or this road in reverse.

Commandant O'Hurley came to the conclusion that the threat existed only from the Dungourney to Clonmult road. His response to this threat involved the ringing of the church bell in Clonmult in the event of British Forces arriving in the village and this was intended to alert the column at the farmhouse.[48] It is not stated in any of the Witness Statements whose responsibility this was. As the church was adjacent to Cronin's public house it is possible that one of the Cronin brothers, who were active in the movement, was to carry out this task.

Commandant O'Hurley dismissed the threat to the upper road because he believed that this road was considered by the British to be too dangerous to travel on.[49] This is an unusual deduction, as I have not found any record of an attack on British forces in the area either prior to or subsequent to the Battle of Clonmult. When troops are in a fixed position, as the column was in this case, it is fundamental that preparations are made to resist the enemy from any direction from which they may attack. Tactical drills need to be rehearsed so that reaction to attack is immediate, ensuring a successful outcome.

The farmhouse, when it was first occupied by the column, was at least adequate for their survival and offered basic living conditions. It afforded protection from the elements and was big enough to house, on average, twenty men. There was a ready supply of water and the local population were generous in providing supplies. Cronin's and Bob Murray's public houses proved useful for obtaining provisions.[50] It appears that when Commandant O'Hurley was looking at the security of the area, he overlooked the design of the farmhouse and its shortcomings with regards to the lack of a back door and lack of firing ports in the walls.

The farmhouse was approximately forty feet long (13 m.), with an outhouse at either end. It had three doors at the front of the building, facing south. The middle door led into the area occupied by the column, the other two to outhouses, which were not connected with the accommodation area. This accommodation area, which consisted of three rooms, had three windows at the front and one small window at the rear. In the attic space there was one small room, which was accessed by a ladder.[51] A major disadvantage was the lack of a door at the rear of the house.

Neither of the gables were accessible.[52] The rear wall was running parallel with and approximately ten feet (3 m.) from a low ditch.[53] The roof of the accommodation was thatched and the roof of the outhouses was slate. There was a grove of approximately twenty trees on the eastern end of the building. On the western side, a haggard ran at right angles to the farmhouse.

The normal procedure in such circumstances would have been to improve the defensiveness of the house by digging at the very least, holes between rooms, also firing-loopholes and escape holes out through the rear wall. As 'Sonny' O'Leary and James Glavin later found out during the battle, there was no point in digging these when under fire and the house surrounded. The fact that this work was not undertaken meant that there was no way out except through the front door and also, those inside were unable to bring down effective fire on the British troops due to a lack of firing ports.

The defence and security of the column within the immediate vicinity of the farmhouse was the responsibility of the column itself. On occasions when a flying column was billeted in an area for a short stay, the local Volunteer Company usually provided sentries, thus enabling all members of the column to sleep securely. As was the case at Clonmult, when the column was billeted in the area for a considerable period, the sentries were detailed from the column members. However, part of the security plan would involve the local Volunteer Company coming to the assistance of the column should the need arise.[54]

To quote Vice-Commandant J. Aherne:

When the column entered a company area instructions were issued that if the column happened to be surrounded the local company or companies were to mobilise all available men and come to their aid. In Cloyne [when the column was surrounded in Bertie Walsh's house, 12th of Dec., 1920] these arrangements worked well as Ladysbridge and Cloyne and a portion of the Aghada Companies were actually converging on Cloyne when the column fought their way out.[55]

On the Sunday afternoon when the column did find itself trapped, no support was forthcoming from the local Company. I emphasise Sunday because it would be expected that the local members would have been at home and thus in a position to render assistance. Considering the lack of strength of the assaulting force of British troops, it is conceivable that a little distraction from the local members could have made the difference.

Commandant O'Hurley was in a predicament, because, while on the one hand he had to plan for a situation where the column may be trapped in the house, at the same time he would have known that his priority would be to escape entrapment, as had almost occurred at Bertie Walsh's house in Cloyne, on Sunday morning the 12th of December.

To quote Capt Paddy Whelan:

> If enemy troops arrived, it was anticipated that their presence would become known to us in advance, and I know it was Diarmuid O'Hurley's intention, in such circumstances, to evacuate the building and give battle outside.[56]

The time spent at Clonmult was used to give the members of the column an opportunity for some concentrated training and specifically to plan and prepare for a second attack on Castlemartyr R.I.C. Barracks. This barracks had been captured previously, but, due to it being located between two dwelling houses the I.R.A. decided not to destroy it. The training would have included lessons on military tactics, signalling, first-aid and the use of explosives. As all members of the column had battle experience, shooting practice was deemed unnecessary. During this time there was a constant turnover of men; as some returned to their Company locations they were replaced by other men. Cobh men, Jack O'Connell, James Aherne, Pat O'Sullivan and Maurice Moore joined the column during the two weeks prior to the battle.

The men were finalising their planned attack on Castlemartyr R.I.C. Barracks, when a dispatch was received from the Adjutant of the First Brigade, Major Florrie O'Donoghue, asking them to attack a military train at Cobh Cross. The dispatch ended with the words, 'if you are unable to carry out the job, please let me know immediately and I will make other arrangements'. The suggestion that the column may not be capable of undertaking this mission greatly annoyed the officers who read it. In the past, assistance from the First Brigade was limited, further fuelling their anger, 'The only help we received from the brigade during the whole period was a gift of 48 lbs. of gelignite and a small exploder'.[57]

The last few days were spent preparing for the move out. Arrangements were made for the column to be billeted at Dooneen, near Leamlara on Sunday night, the 20th of February. On Friday, 18th of February, the I.R.A. entered the house of P.H. Barry, at Ballyadam, near Carrigtwohill. They removed beds, bedding, delph, jewellery and seven pounds in cash.[58] The owner was opposed to the I.R.A. and had refused to subscribe to its upkeep. This house was only a few miles from Dooneen and it is possible that the items were required to furnish the new billet for the column.

On Saturday, 19th of February, the day before the battle, some of the column members went to Dungourney for confession. Jack O'Connell stated that this was when the informer, who was an ex-soldier, was out trapping rabbits and he observed the volunteers coming through Clonmult on their return from Dungourney.[59]

On the Sunday morning, Dick Hegarty was at home at Moanroe, Garryvoe, just finishing a few days leave from the column. He was taken to Clonmult in a ginnet and trap, driven by his uncle Michael Kennefick and accompanied by his brother Jack.[60] After dropping Dick off in Clonmult village at about 2.00 p.m., the two men while on their way home saw two truck loads of Auxiliaries in Castlemartyr. There is a good chance that these were the same auxiliaries that reinforced the British troops in Clonmult that evening.[61]

John Harty and his friend Edmond Terry, who were both members of Na Fianna, the I.R.A. youth organisation, met in Churchtown South after mass on the morning of the battle. It had been arranged that they would take funds that had been collected from the farmers in their area, to the column headquarters, which was a collection point for such monies. This money was levied from farmers and used as a war chest by the I.R.A. It was also arranged that they would bring cigarettes and clean laundry for the I.R.A. men. While on their way to Clonmult they met two of their friends in Ladysbridge, Robert Walsh of Ballycotton and William Garde, who may not have been members of Na Fianna.[62] They cycled to Clonmult, arriving there just before Dick Hegarty. They stopped at the crossroads in Clonmult village and Edmond Terry took the opportunity to visit his grandmother. While the other three were waiting outside, Dick Hegarty arrived. They waited for Edmond Terry and the five set off for the farmhouse, approximately one mile away.

The reconnaissance group

The composition and activities of the reconnaissance group that departed the farmhouse at Clonmult sometime between 2.00 p.m. and 3.00 p.m. on that Sunday afternoon, deserves careful analysis.[63] The mission of the reconnaissance group was to carry out an inspection of Cobh Junction railway station. The column had been tasked by First Brigade Headquarters in Cork city to carry out an attack on a military convoy, conveying explosives by rail from Cobh to Cork on the following Tuesday, the 22nd or Wednesday, the 23rd of February.[64] Previous accounts have given different timings, even different dates for the departure but the details here are now confirmed from the Witness Statements.

The initial reconnaissance group consisted of the Column Commander Commandant O'Hurley and Vice-Commandant Joseph Aherne. Aherne's second in command Capt. Paddy Whelan was to be left in charge of the column being the next senior officer. However, neither of the two officers were familiar with the area around Cobh Junction railway station, therefore, Paddy Whelan, who was familiar with the terrain, was included in the reconnaissance group at short notice.[65]

When they were leaving, Capt. Jack O'Connell of Cobh was appointed as acting Column Commander over the head of Capt. Paddy Higgins, who was senior to Capt. Jack O'Connell. This led to friction between the two officers and a conflict of command. Capt. O'Connell was ordered by Commandant O'Hurley to vacate the farmhouse at 6 o'clock that evening and march the column to Dooneen, Leamlara, and their new safe house.

The reconnaissance group left the area in a Ford car. When they had driven down to the 'T' junction, where they could have turned left and up past Clonmult Church to Cronin's pub, a debate started between O'Hurley and Ahern about going up to Bob Murray's who had a public house in Clonmult, to thank him for his hospitality, now that they were leaving the area for some time.[66] They eventually decided against going up there as they could not afford the time delay that would result from further hospitality which was almost certain to be extended by the publican. Had they decided to go to Murray's, it would have meant that they would still have been in the area when the attack on the farmhouse commenced. Having these three men in the area, but outside of the British Army cordon around the farmhouse, could have made all the difference to the outcome of the battle. However, this was not to be, they drove through Rathorgan crossroads and on to Cobh Junction which was about fourteen miles to the south.

I now wish to examine the composition of the reconnaissance group. The reconnaissance party consisted of the three most senior officers of the Column. The normal military procedure was that the commander carried out the reconnaissance, accompanied by the necessary advisors, in this instance Capt. Paddy Whelan on account of his familiarity with Cobh Junction. In addition, he would bring along a driver and some riflemen as security. While the Column Commander was carrying out his reconnaissance, his second in command, Vice-Commandant Joseph Aherne, should have been left in charge of the column. By taking so many senior officers along, the column was being stripped of its leadership.

The duty of the second in command in this situation was that he would assume the temporary responsibility of command. He would move the column at the designated time to the location of the rendezvous, as instructed by Commandant O'Hurley. The order was to vacate the farmhouse at 6.00 p.m. and march to new billets at Dooneen, near Leamlara.[67] Here, the reconnaissance party and the remainder of the column would be re-united. With Commandant O'Hurley back in command, Vice-Commandant Aherne would resume his duties as second in command.

The decision to appoint Capt. Jack O'Connell as acting Column Commander over Capt. Paddy Higgins was divisive within the column. The decision to overlook Capt. Paddy Higgins as acting Column Commander appears to have had its origins as far back as the 29th of December, when the column attacked the joint R.I.C./Black and Tan foot patrol on the Main Street of Midleton. Paddy Higgins was with Joseph Aherne's group and Aherne was not impressed by Higgins' lack of effort during the gun battle which left two Black and Tans dead. Joseph Aherne says, 'Higgins on that occasion didn't show any great aptitude for the work, so I decide to pass him over on this occasion'.[68] This is the reason Joseph Aherne gives for Jack O'Connell being appointed as acting officer commanding the column over Higgins.[69] It was therefore, a weakened and divided column that found itself surrounded in the farmhouse at Clonmult.

The British Army at Clonmult

The strength of the British patrol that set out for Clonmult, Co. Cork on Sunday morning, 20th of February, 1920, has been estimated in previous accounts of the battle as being up to Company strength, which would number approximately one hundred and twenty men.[70] Eleven Crossley tenders would have been required to transport such a force. *The Regimental History of the Royal Hampshire Regiment* gives the strength of the patrol as four officers and twenty-one other ranks (soldiers) from the Regiment.[71] Two Crossley tenders were used to transport this force and were driven by two Royal Army Service Corps (R.A.S.C.) drivers, giving a total of twenty-seven personnel. This number plus the informer, who was also taken to Clonmult, both as a guide and hostage, corresponds with the carrying capacity of two Crossley tenders which was fourteen personnel per vehicle including the driver.[72] Local civilians who went to Rathorgan crossroads, where the British parked the vehicles, reported later that there were indeed two Crossley tenders parked there.[73]

There were three officers on patrol from the 2nd Battalion, Hampshire Regiment, Lieut. A.R. Koe, Lieut. G.R.A. Dove, Lieut. D. F. Hook, M.C., and Lieut. H. Hammond, M.C., who was intelligence officer of the 17th Infantry Brigade and was an officer of the Dorsetshire Regiment.[74] The senior N.C.O. was Company Sergeant Major Edward Corney, M.M.

The patrol departed Victoria Barracks in Cork city at 2.15 p.m., under the command of Lieut. Koe. It travelled directly to the Royal Irish Constabulary Barracks, in Midleton. The R.I.C. Barracks, subsequently the old Gárda station, stood on the courthouse side of the present Gárda Station. This was standard procedure to notify the local R.I.C. officer that the army patrol was operating in the vicinity, so as to inform them of their mission and their destination.

From Midleton, the patrol travelled north on the Lisgoold-Fermoy road for approximately one mile, where it turned right, past where the East Cork Oil depot is presently situated. The convoy continued north passing through Elfordstown, taking the right fork beyond where the Earth Station is located. From here it continued on to the Dispensary crossroads, it turned right and travelled directly to Rathorgan crossroads. The total distance from Midleton was approximately ten miles.

When the vehicle patrol arrived at Rathorgan crossroads, it was decided to leave the two tenders there and use the crossroads as a patrol harbour. This location was ideal for parking the two tenders as any attempt to drive the vehicles nearer to the farmhouse, where the column was located, could have cost them the element of surprise. The location was also used to detain the local civilians who came up to investigate the activities of the British troops and who would have alerted the column.

The patrol was now broken down into three groups. The first group consisted of one N.C.O., six soldiers and the two drivers; they were left to guard the vehicles, the informer and to detain any civilians.[75] This group had another very important purpose, in the event of the attacking force meeting overwhelming opposition, they would have been able to withdraw back to the crossroads under covering fire from the soldiers located there. The second group consisted of Lieut. Koe, Lieut. Hammond, M.C., C.S.M. Corney, M.M. and seven soldiers, the third group was, Lieut. Hook, Lieut. Dove and six soldiers. The two latter groups made up the attacking force; they were now ready to set off and investigate the activities at the farmhouse.[76]

CHAPTER 2

The Battle of Clonmult

When Dick Hegarty and the four cyclists, William Garde, John Harty, Robert Walsh and Edmond Terry arrived at the farmhouse, on the Sunday afternoon, they brought the number of I.R.A. men to seventeen, in addition to the four cyclists. As they arrived they met John Joe Joyce and Michael Desmond who were walking to the well to fill water bottles.[77] The well was approximately forty yards east of the house and is still in use today. The time was somewhere between three and four o'clock in the afternoon. Paddy Whelan and Diarmuid (Sonny) O'Leary give the time of the first shots as 3.00 p.m., while Jack O' Connell and Paddy Whelan give the time as being 4.00 p.m.

Dick Hegarty and the four cyclists had just reached the farmyard when they heard a shout to get inside the house to safety. Diarmuid O'Leary was looking out one of the windows and suddenly spotted the British soldiers:

> I chanced to look out a front window and saw, to my amazement, soldiers crawling past the gateway near the boreen. The time was now about 3.00 p.m. I immediately gave the alarm and, almost at once, the military opened fire on us from all sides.[78]

This would have been at the same time as Michael Desmond and John-Joe Joyce, became engaged in a gun battle with the British soldiers who were beginning to surround the house. This group, under Lieut. Koe, had approached the house from the south and had reached their destination before the remainder of the troops who approached from the west.[79] The two I.R.A. men were each armed with only a revolver, and would have been both outgunned and outnumbered by the British. This one-sided engagement was quickly over. Michael Desmond died near the well. John Joe Joyce, though mortally wounded, managed to crawl back to the window at the rear of the house and call to those inside, telling them that the house was surrounded.[80] John Joe Joyce died so near to the house that his body was partially burnt by the burning thatch from the roof.

The Volunteers were now in the worst possible predicament. They had been taken by surprise because their two sentries had left their posts.[81] Their ability to return effective fire on the British was greatly reduced owing to a lack of firing positions, which should have been constructed during their long stay in the location. The lack of at least one other exit was also a major handicap. A secondary exit should have been knocked out of the rear wall during their period of occupation. A crawl hole would have sufficed. The only course of action open to the trapped column was an aggressive breakout and this would have to be attempted before the British troops established their positions. After about an hours' firing Capt. Jack O'Connell, the officer in charge, assessed the situation and came to the conclusion that the prospects of fighting a winning battle from within the house were absolutely hopeless and decided on attempting a breakout.[82] However, a command conflict arose between him and Capt. Paddy Higgins, who was still annoyed at being passed over by Jack O'Connell and was not inclined to charge out of the house against the British rifles. This was when the absence of the real second–in–command was to cost the column dearly. It was a time for quick decisions, clear orders and complete obedience. It was not the occasion for disagreement between the two senior officers present.

The result was that only four men agreed to attempt a breakout with Capt. O'Connell. These were Capt. James Aherne, Capt. Dick Hegarty, Capt. Diarmuid O'Leary and Vol. Michael Hallihan. Capt. O'Connell now distributed the reserve ammunition and some grenades.[83] Firing was intensified from the house in order to provide covering fire for the men who were about to attempt to breakout. With only three windows and one door at the front of the building, the lack of firing ports and a restricted field of fire, greatly reduced the ability of the remaining men to give accurate and effective support to the four attempting the breakout. Around this time the men started singing 'The Soldiers Song' as an act of defiance.[84]

Capt. O'Connell, armed with a rifle with bayonet fixed, was the first out through the door and seemingly caught the British troops by surprise. He ran across the yard to a gateway. As he turned up to the right, he was fired on by two soldiers from the corner of a field, bordering the western side of the haggard. He returned fire, wounding one and the other ran back. It appears that the wounded man was Company Sergeant Major Edward Corney M.M. and the second man was Lieut. Koe.[85] He ran further down a track and when he looked around for his companions, to his amazement, he was alone.

Vol. Michael Hallihan had followed his officer and he was shot dead immediately outside the door. Capt. James Aherne followed and managed to cover approximately two-hundred yards, before being shot dead while climbing over a ditch. What he would not have been aware of was that he was running in the direction of the crossroads, where the Crossley tenders were parked and would have been killed or captured had he reached them. Capt. Dick Hegarty was next out, but was shot down and mortally wounded while attempting to reach the fence in front of the house. The last man out was Capt. Diarmuid (Sonny) O'Leary, he managed to reach the comparative safety of the haggard: [86]

"I got into the haggard, but, seeing the other boys fall, decided there was no hope of escape and dashed back again into the house amidst a hail of bullets, none of which, fortunately hit me".

There is a possibility that the dying Capt. Dick Hegarty was still managing to fire his rifle and this may have distracted the troops enough for Capt. O'Leary to get back into the house.[87] The attempted breakout was over – of the five, three were dead and only one got through the British cordon.

The British officer in charge, Lieut. Koe, assessing the situation from his perspective, appears to have concluded that while the I.R.A. column was trapped, he himself did not have an adequate force with which to overwhelm the garrison in a frontal assault. He must also have been concerned that they were liable to be attacked by I.R.A. forces outside the cordon. His plan was to maintain the cordon around the house and also to send three soldiers back to the crossroads to order one of the drivers to go to Midleton in search of bombs and reinforcements. Capt. Jack O'Connell, who had survived the breakout, saw the soldiers crossing the fields in the direction of the crossroads. He fired on them but they did not reply as their mission was to reach the crossroads safely.

Inside the house, Capt. Paddy Higgins, was now in charge of a greatly reduced Column. Three of the senior officers were gone on a reconnaissance, five of their comrades had been killed during the last hour and at that stage some were convinced that Jack O'Connell may also be dead or captured and they themselves were still surrounded. Capt. Higgins decided to continue the fight from inside, hoping that some help might reach them. An aspect of the column's security plan was that the members of the local Volunteer Company would come to their assistance in the event of the British forces attacking them. Unfortunately, for the column, no assistance appeared to be forthcoming. They were on their own.

An attempt was now made to breach one of the walls of the house. Paddy Higgins says that it was a gable wall while Diarmuid O'Leary says it was the rear wall. As neither gable was accessible it was more than likely, the rear wall. Bayonets, knives and forks were used to remove the stones etc. and eventually a hole was opened large enough for a man to crawl through.[88] Diarmuid O'Leary was first to attempt to get through, but, as soon as he put his head through the opening, he was spotted, he received a bullet wound in the head and had to be pulled back inside by his comrades. He soon lapsed into unconsciousness as a result of his wound.

When the British Army driver, who was sent to Midleton for reinforcements, arrived there, he found that two truckloads of Auxiliaries, who were travelling between Youghal and Cork, were at the R.I.C. Barracks. A number of accounts identify a truckload of Black and Tans as the reinforcements. Black and Tans are often confused for Auxiliaries and visa versa. Black and Tans did not travel around by the truckload, they were sent in small numbers as replacements and reinforcements to R.I.C. Barracks and were under the immediate command of the local R.I.C. sergeant.[89] It was the Auxiliaries who generally travelled around in trucks and therefore, it was almost certainly members of this force that provided the reinforcements for the troops at Clonmult. It was also standard procedure that all British convoys would consist of at least two vehicles. This gives an indication of how many Auxiliaries travelled to Clonmult. When reinforcements were sought, it is my conclusion that some R.I.C. and Black and Tans from the town also travelled to the battle scene.

On several occasions during the battle, the British called on the besieged men to surrender. The I.R.A. men were not going to give themselves up as their future prospects would have been very bleak. Just about nine weeks previously, on the 11th of December 1920, the British authorities had declared Martial Law in the counties of Cork, Kerry, Limerick and Tipperary.[90] As a coincidence, the first official reprisals under Martial Law were carried out in Midleton.[91] It was also decreed that: 'Any unauthorised person found in possession of arms, ammunition or explosives would on conviction of a military court, suffer death'.

On the 1st of February, just three weeks prior to Clonmult, Capt. Con Murphy from Millstreet was executed in Cork, after being found in possession of a revolver. This was the likely fate hanging over the besieged men.

Twenty-four police reinforcements, under the command of an R.I.C. County Inspector, arrived at Rathorgan crossroads and parked there. They then proceeded across the fields and arrived at the farmhouse at about 5.30 p.m.[92] The Auxiliaries were positioned on the western side of the house and at the end of the barn.[93] They had brought petrol with them and without delay, an army officer proceeded to set fire to the thatch roof of the farmhouse using the petrol and grenades. I have come to the conclusion that the officer who set fire to the roof was Lieut. H. Hammond, M.C., who was intelligence officer of the 17th Infantry Brigade and was an officer of the Dorsetshire Regiment.[94] When the sound and smell of the burning thatch reached the I.R.A. men they knew that this was the beginning of the end. Diarmuid O'Leary recalled 'we were getting sick from inhaling the fumes'. A British Army officer was contacted and promised that their lives would be saved if the remainder of the column surrendered.[95] This promise was highlighted later during the courts-martial.

The decision was taken to surrender approximately fifteen minutes after the roof was set on fire. Capt. Paddy Higgins ordered the men to throw their weapons into the fire prior to surrendering.[96] Following this, nine men came out of the house to surrender. Seventeen year old John Harty, who was first out of the house, was felled by being clubbed in between his eyes with the brass plated butt of a service rifle; this actually saved his life, as he was on the ground when the killing started. The others were lined up alongside the wall of the haggard with their hands up. Immediately the Auxiliaries set upon them. The Auxiliaries moved down the line and shot every man. Lieut. Christopher O'Sullivan, Vols. David Desmond, Jeremiah Aherne and his first-cousin Liam Aherne, Donal Dennehy, Joseph Morrissey and James Glavin were shot dead. Capt. Paddy Higgins recalled 'a Tan put his revolver to my mouth and fired, I felt as if I was falling through a bottomless pit. Then I thought I heard a voice saying "This fellow is not dead, we will finish him off"'. Only for a military officer coming along, I, too, would be gone'. The arrival of the Army officer ended the killing spree.

Luckily for the remaining men, they were delayed in exiting the house, as they were attempting to carry the wounded and semi-conscious Diarmuid O'Leary out and this delay saved their lives. They came out after the British officer had regained control. The second group were Maurice Moore and Patrick O'Sullivan who carried Diarmuid O'Leary. These were followed by Robert Walsh, Edmond Terry and William Garde.[97] These men were ordered into the haggard where they were detained and searched.

The Battle of Clonmult was now over. Twelve I.R.A. men were dead, eight wounded and only one had escaped.[98] The British casualty list was two military and three police men wounded of which one soldier and one policeman were severely wounded.

The British often refer to Clonmult as Kilmichael in reverse, because, at Kilmichael the I.R.A. under General Tom Barry claimed that the Auxiliaries made a false surrender during the engagement. The British have claimed that at Clonmult the I.R.A. made a false surrender and this is their reason for the killing of the I.R.A. men.[99] Their claim is that after the first group came out of the house those remaining inside began firing.[100]

When Capt Paddy Higgins decided to surrender, a decision was made to throw their weapons into the burning house; this in itself would have resulted in the ammunition 'cooking off' in the heat. This is one possible theory that I am putting forward for shots to be heard from the house. The other possibility is that the British were just attempting to cover up their tracks with falsehoods. Capt. Higgins is quite clear that he had a revolver placed to his mouth and some of the others were shot just below the eyes, which also leads me to conclude that they were shot from a very close range. Finally, if fire was reopened on the British after the initial group surrendered, why is it that none of the British were injured?

The wounded C.S.M., Edward Corney was taken to Carey's house on the main road and while he was there waiting for transport, two of the Carey brothers, Moss and Mike, together with

Mikey Sullivan, stole his blood-stained tunic and ran off with it. After removing the aide-memoire from the pocket they stuffed the tunic down a rabbit burrow. The Hampshires conducted an extensive search for the aide–memoire as it contained sensitive military information, but they failed in their quest.[101]

When Capt. Jack O'Connell made his successful escape from the farmhouse, he ran down a boreen which ran in a southerly direction for approximately two-hundred yards. This boreen is now overgrown. As stated earlier, he was astonished to find that none of his comrades were with him. He returned to within sight of the farmhouse and considered attempting to get back inside.[102] He realised that two soldiers had been detailed to pursue him and this forced him to abandon both his intention to get back inside the farmhouse and his present location. He decided to make an attempt to locate some of the local volunteers and with these, his intention was to attack the British troops from their rear and thus relieve the besieged column. He eventually met two local Volunteers, Willie Foley and Johnny Lawton.[103] One, he sent for arms, the other he wanted to take back to the farmhouse. The individual showed extreme reluctance and eventually decided to accompany the other Volunteer to fetch the weapons from the graveyard.[104] The weapons belonging to the local Clonmult Volunteers were buried in the old cemetery in the town-land of Ballyeightragh which was only just across the valley approximately one mile east of the battle site.[105] Neither of these two individuals returned to Clonmult prior to Jack O'Connell's departure later that evening.

Another local volunteer arrived at the scene on a bicycle. Jack O'Connell did not realise at the time that this man was the captain of the local (Clonmult) Company.[106] He informed Jack that the A.S.U. of the North East Cork Battalion was located near the village of Ballynoe, six miles to the north, and he suggested going and getting help from them.[107] This A.S.U. did get to Clonmult much later that evening but, by then the battle was over. They came as far as Gurteen crossroads, just over a mile north east of the battle site.[108] Jack O'Connell waited in vain for the two volunteers to return with the weapons. He was also kept busy dodging the attention of two British soldiers who were following him. He finally saw the thatched roof on fire and he eventually left the area at about 6.30 p.m. when silence descended and he knew in his heart that the battle was over. He made his way to Knockraha which was about fourteen miles away.[109]

At about this time, the British forces would also have been making preparations to depart Clonmult. Now that the battle was over, their concern was to depart before any I.R.A. forces would arrive. Weapons, ammunition and hand grenades were recovered from the burning house and all similar items were collected from the dead bodies. The eight prisoners were kept together and the entire body of both British and Irish forces trekked across the fields and back to the crossroads where the vehicles were parked. The bodies of the twelve I.R.A. men were left where they had fallen. It is of interest that all travel between the crossroads and the farmhouse during the afternoon was across the fields. Even when the battle was over the British did not bring their vehicles down the road to the battle scene. This was standard procedure, as by doing so they would have been travelling into unknown territory and risking an ambush. When all of the troops, Auxiliaries and I.R.A. men were loaded onto the vehicles, the convoy made its way to Midleton by the reverse route that they had used earlier that day.

When the reconnaissance party left Clonmult, they travelled directly to Killacloyne, which is situated approximately two miles on the west side of Carrigtwohill, on the old road to Cork. Just before they reached Killacloyne bridge, they turned north on to the Knockraha road and parked the car just off the junction. They proceeded to walk from the car to Cobh Junction railway station along the railway track. Having completed their reconnaissance they returned to the car with the intention of driving to the agreed rendezvous with their column at Dooneen. Dooneen is a town-land about four miles north of Carrigtwohill near the village of Leamlara.[110] While the three men were at Cobh Junction, six or seven British Army trucks passed them heading for Cork city. The men were convinced, in hindsight, that this was the same convoy that was transporting the remnants of their column as captives to Victoria Barracks.

On approaching the car, they realised that Capt. Michael Burke, of the Cobh Company was waiting for them.[111] This in itself was not unusual, as it had been agreed that the column would be reinforced by Volunteers from the Cobh Company for the proposed attack on the British at Cobh Junction on the following Tuesday. However, Michael Burke had met an unnamed Volunteer while on his way to Killacloyne, and had been informed that there had been a battle at Clonmult.[112] Michael Burke's wife was a sister of Capt. James Ahern, who had been killed that afternoon at Clonmult. Commandant O'Hurley concluded that if anyone had managed to escape from Clonmult, they would make their way to Knockraha. Capt. Paddy Whelan guessed that any survivor would make his way to Canavan's house in Knockraha.[113] They decided to drive there and on entering the village they met Capt. Jack O'Connell and he was with Capt. Martin Corry, who was O.C. of the local I.R.A. Company.[114]

Jack O'Connell gave them as much information as he had but at this stage he himself was not aware of the extent of the defeat at Clonmult. He would only have been aware of the deaths of four men. The four men decided to drive back to Clonmult 'in case some of the Volunteers were still holding out.'[115] As O'Hurley remarked 'if we cannot save them we can die with them.'[116] They, like the British, parked their car on the roadway some distance from the farmhouse and travelled across the fields. When they arrived at the site the only sound was the crackling of the still burning house.[117]

After the British had left the scene, some of the locals ventured to the battle site. They were accompanied by the local Catholic curate, Fr. Curtin, who rendered the spiritual assistance of the Catholic Church on the bodies of the dead men.[118] Lt. Ahern and Volunteer Staunton, both of the Dungourney Company were at the scene when they arrived.[119] The twelve bodies had been collected and placed beside each other with their faces covered with canvas; this was how they were found by their comrades, at about midnight when they returned.

Capt. Paddy Whelan best describes the harrowing scene:

> I undertook the heartbreaking task of uncovering their faces and identifying them, calling out each consecutively. This sad task took me some time, but between sobs of anguish, I managed it. There were two distinct pauses as I went along the row, as I had great difficulty in naming Liam Aherne (Jos. Aherne's brother) and Jerry Aherne (first cousin of Jos.) I will not even attempt to describe the mental anguish of Diarmuid O'Hurley. All four of us – Diarmuid, Jos., Jacko and myself – sobbed with a terrible grief and sense of loss at the fate that had befallen our beloved comrades, some four or five of whom had bullet holes in the face, just below their eyes, where they had been shot by the Tans whilst prisoners. There was nothing we could do but cover their faces again, and take our sad departure to Leamlara.[120]

The four men spent that night in Fr. Francis Flannery's house in Midleton. The distraught Jack O'Connell was consoled by Capt. Paddy Whelan:

> That night, Jacko (Jack O'Connell) and I shared a bed. I remember putting my arm around him, to give some comfort and consolation. I believe – and told him so – that he had done all that was humanly possible to save the Column.[121]

When all of the troops, police and prisoners were loaded onto the vehicles at the crossroads, the convoy set out for Midleton. I have concluded that at least one vehicle left earlier for Midleton to prepare for the arrival of the prisoners. This is because members of the Royal Irish Constabulary interrupted that evening's show at the cinema, cleared the building and ordered the patrons to go home, before the prisoners arrived at the R.I.C. barracks. The cinema, which was located at the northern end of the town, adjacent to where the Clonmult monument now stands, was near the R.I.C. barracks. At this stage, word of the battle was beginning to filter into the town and the authorities did not want a crowd in the vicinity of the Constabulary barracks when the prisoners arrived there.

The principal reason for taking the prisoners to Midleton was to have them identified. However, only Capt Paddy Higgins was identified. Diarmuid O'Leary gave a false name and this later caused some confusion for his family. Shortly afterwards, the prisoners were put back on the trucks and transferred to Victoria Barracks in Cork city. As the prisoners were being put on the trucks in Midleton, they overheard the soldiers being ordered to shoot them should any attempt be made to rescue them.

Volunteers Dan Cashman and Jack Aherne were on week-end leave from the column and both spent the Sunday in Ballinacurra, two kilometres south of Midleton, drilling and training the local Company. That night when they came into Midleton they saw lorries with military and police drawn up outside the R.I.C. Barracks.

Dan Cashman stated:[122]

Jack suggested that we would go out on the Cork road and ambush them. We collected another Volunteer named Joe Kinsella, went out the road about a mile and a half and hurriedly built a barricade of stones on the road. We then got inside the hedge and waited for the lorries. When the military came along we blazed into them with revolvers. They burst through the barricade firing as they went and continued on to Cork. We had no idea then (about 9.00 p.m.) that the lorries contained some of our boys captured in Clonmult a few hours previously, nor had we any idea that the Column had been practically wiped out. That night we stayed at a farmer's house at Ballinacurra and it was there we learned what had happened at Clonmult, from the woman of the house.

The remainder of the journey to Cork was uneventful and the prisoners were lodged in the Barracks. The wounded Paddy Higgins and Diarmuid O'Leary were taken to the garrison hospital. O'Leary recalls waking up from his unconscious state while having his hair shaved in preparation for his head wound being attended to. Paddy Higgins had his mouth wound attended to, but the head of the bullet, that had lodged in his upper jaw remained there. It fell out a few days later while he was sitting beside the fire in the prison. 'It was a lead bullet, not a nickel one.'[123] Had it been a nickel bullet he would not have survived.

The British captured a substantial quantity of weapons, ammunition and grenades. The armament of the column consisted of 17 rifles, 3 shotguns, 15 revolvers, six grenades and about 1,000 rounds of ammunition.[124] The weapons and ammunition of the reconnaissance group, the rifle taken by Jack O'Connell and the ammunition expended during the battle can be deducted from the columns arms and represents the list of equipment captured. This is mentioned in the British military communiqué, issued on Sunday evening from Dublin. However, in their second communiqué, issued on the Monday and published on Tuesday morning, it stated that the military also captured a car. Jim Hegarty, a surviving witness to the battle, in an interview with me, also stated that he remembers the British burning a car in the farm yard that evening.[125]

There were 13 rifles and carbines, 12 revolvers, 198 rounds of service ammunition, a Mills bomb, 2 shot-guns, bayonets and equipment captured by the British Army following the battle.[126]

CHAPTER 3

The funerals

On Monday morning, the National newspapers gave brief details of the battle and stated thirteen as the number of I.R.A. men killed.[127] However, due to the confusion of the battle, it is understandable that this incorrect figure was given. In reality, twelve I.R.A. men had been killed, whose bodies had been left overnight beside the smouldering ruin of what had been their billet at Clonmult. The British troops returned for the bodies on Monday morning and carried out a more thorough search of the immediate area. They were convinced that the body of the column commander had been removed by the I.R.A. during the night, this gave rise to the figure of thirteen killed. The bodies were conveyed to Victoria Barracks. For the remainder of the week following the battle, the British were active around Clonmult searching and interrogating suspects.[128]

Information on the battle gradually reached the families of the column members on Sunday night and Monday morning. The mother of the two Desmond brothers, Michael and David, was very ill in bed at her home in Midleton. At about 6.00 p.m., her daughters who were in an adjacent room heard her speaking to someone. They went to her bedroom to find that she was alone, they asked her who she was speaking to. She told them that she had been speaking with David and Michael, but everything was alright, they were with God. The family of Christopher O'Sullivan saw his bicycle in the back of an Army truck, when it was passing through Midleton. Dick Hegarty's younger sister heard that her brother was dead when she was called out from her classroom. The distress endured by all of these families resonated throughout the community.

During the day, a special meeting of Midleton U.D.C. was held and a vote of sympathy was passed to the families of the deceased.[129] At about 11 a.m., Tuesday, businesses in the town began to close and put up their shutters. That afternoon, a military party patrolled the town and insisted that the shops must re-open. This was done, but no business was transacted.[130] Likewise, the members of Cobh U.D.C. passed a vote of sympathy and expressed their condolences to the families of two Cobh men, Vol. James Glavin, and Capt. James Ahern, who had been elected to the town council for Sinn Féin the previous year. James Glavin's father wrote to the Council: 'it is a source of consolation to us to realise that our son gave his life, in company with his gallant and brave companions, many of whom were natives of Cobh, for our dear country.'[131]

The following day, Wednesday, 23rd of February, the bodies were released to their families and were removed from Victoria Barracks late that evening. The cortege carrying the twelve coffins, travelled together as far as Cobh Cross and from here the coffins of James Ahern and James Glavin were taken to St. Colman's Cathedral in Cobh. The other ten coffins were taken to Midleton by lorry, where they arrived at about 10.00 p.m. 'Crowds had been gathering in the town from 4.00 p.m. and the church bell had been ringing since about that time. It was a fine, dry, calm night, though somewhat cold, and a deep silence pervading the whole scene at such an hour at night, the event was undoubtedly solemn, and was one calculated never to be forgotten by those who were present on the sad occasion.'[132] The coffins were shouldered from the Cork side of the town to the church, where they were placed in front of the high alter.

Following Requiem High Mass at 10 a.m. on Thursday, the nine coffins of the local men were laid to rest in the Republican Plot. The coffins were draped in tricolours and there were innumerable wreaths.[133] The tenth coffin, Dick Hegarty's, was conveyed to

1. Composite photograph of the fourteen men who lost their lives as a result of the Battle of Clonmult. From left to right, back row: Capt. Richard Hegarty, Vol. Jermiah Aherne, Lt. Christopher O'Sullivan, Vol. Joseph Morrissey, Vol. Michael Hallihan, and Lt. Patrick O'Sullivan. Middle row: Vol. James Glavin, Vol. John Joe Joyce, Capt. James Ahern, Vol. Michael Desmond. Front Row: Vol. Donal Dennehy, Vol. Liam Aherne, Vol. David Desmond, Vol. Maurice Moore.

2. Ruin of house at Garrylaurence, after massacre.

3. Ruin of house at Garrylaurence, Clonmult where the Flying Column were massacred on Sunday, 20 February, 1921.

4. Captain Paddy Whelan, Cobh.

5. Vice Comdt. Joe Aherne, Midleton.

6. Cronin's Bar, Clonmult.

7. Vol. Dan Cashman, Midleton. He was in Walsh's house in Cloyne and now resides in Dublin. Photo taken at Conway's farm house near Garryvoe.

8. Left to right: Comdt. Joe Ahern Midleton, Vol. Dick Hegarty, Garryvoe, killed at Clonmult by Crown Forces, Capt. Paddy Higgins, Ballinrostig, Aghada. Captured at Clonmult, shot by Black & Tan after surrendering but survived and was sentenced to death. The Truce, July 11th, 1921, saved Paddy from execution. He died in 2004 in Dublin and donated his body to a medical college.

9. Mr. Patrick Higgins, one of the Clonmult survivors, shown seated between his parents in this picture taken after his release. In the back row are the men who conveyed him to his home after he was released. There was some fear that he would be re-arrested to circumvent the legal decision advised to his solicitor, Mr. William J. Barry, of Midleton.

10. The ruin of the farmhouse at Clonmult following the battle.

11. The ruin of the farmhouse from a different angle.

12. Vol. David Desmond, Midleton. Shot at Clonmult after surrendering. He was the brother of Vol. Michael Desmond, Clonmult, also shot at Clonmult. Michael was with Vol. John Joe Joyce, Middleton, when surprised by Military and both were mortally wounded.

13. Captain Paddy Whelan, Cobh.

14. Vol. Jimmy Glavin, shot by Black and Tan after surrendering. He threw his rifle back into the fire rather than hand it up to the Tans.

15. Vol. Christopher O'Sullivan, Midleton, shot at Clonmult, February 20th, 1921, uncle of O'Connor, Chemist, Midleton.

16. Vol. Dan Cashman, Midleton. He was in Walshs' house in Cloyne and now resides in Dublin. Photo taken at Conway's farmhouse near Garryvoe.

17. Vol. Jimmy Glavin, Cobh, shot at Clonmult. This photo was taken at Conway's, Garryvoe where the Column was staying after the escape from Cloyne.

18. Robert Walsh (background). One of the four youths captured at Clonmult.

19. The Republican plot in Midleton's Holy Rosary Church.

20. John Joe Joyce, 16 Main St. Middleton. Born 28/08/1898, Middleton Co. Cork. Killed 20/02/1921 at Clonmult, Co. Cork. Engineering student University College Cork.

21. Photo taken at Clonmult Graveyard 1961. Left – Right: John Harty, Diarmuid O'Leary, Paddy Higgins, Edmund Terry.

22. Men of the 4th Battallion, Cork No. 1 Brigade, I.R.A. Left to right: Michael Desmond★, Paddy Higgins, James Glavin★, Donal Dennehy★, Joseph Aherne, Richard Hegarty★, Joseph Morrissey★, Michael Hallihan★, David Stanton, Patrick White.

★ Killed during the Battle of Clonmult.

23. Four of the men captured at Clonmult, clockwise from top left: Robert Walsh, John Harty, Edmund Terry, William Garde.

24. Comdt. Diarmuid O'Hurley, column commander at Clonmult, killed in action with Crown Forces, at Gortacrue, north of Midleton, on the morning of 28th of May, 1921.

25. 1917 – 1921 I.R.A. Service Medal: This medal was awarded to I.R.A. combatants who took part in military operations against the Crown Forces between 1917 and the 11th of July, 1921, the day of the truce. The 'Comrac' (Warrior) bar was not on the medal awarded to non combatants such as the Cumann na mBan and na Fíanna. The medal was awarded, officially named and numbered to all I.R.A. men who were killed during the War of Independence as well as to those who were entitled to the medal but had died prior to its presentation in 1941. All other recipients received the medal unnamed.

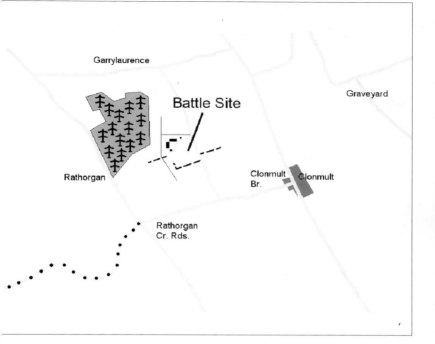

26. *Above:* Map of Clonmult Area.

27. *Right:* Map of Route Taken By Crown Forces to Clonmult.

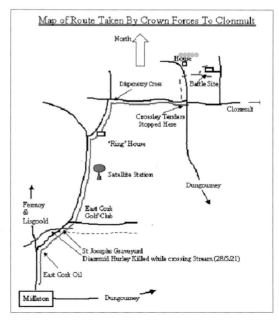

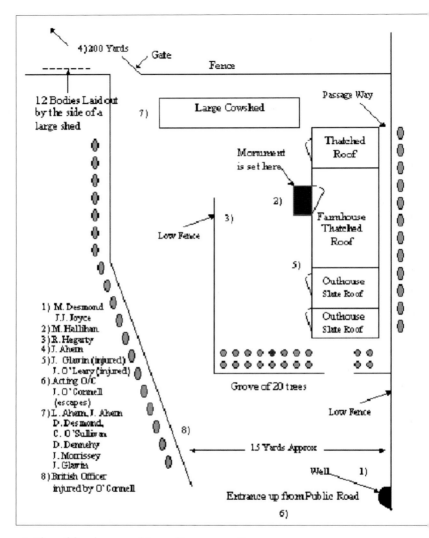

28. Plan of farmhouse and immediate surrounding area.

Ballymacoda, near Youghal. At 3 p.m. on the same day, the funerals of the two Cobh men were held in Cobh Cathedral and they were buried in the Republican Plot in the old graveyard at Ticknock, on the northern side of the town. On Friday, Dick Hegarty was laid to rest beside the church in Ballymacoda.

Diarmuid O'Hurley, Joseph Aherne, Paddy Whelan and Jack O'Connell spent the Monday night in Midleton, in Fr. Francis Flannery's house and on the Thursday, attended the funerals.[134] 'When the internment had been completed, O'Hurley drew his gun, signalled to Paddy Whelan and O'Connell to do likewise, and we then gave our last salute by firing three volleys over the grave. We then made our way quickly out of the graveyard.'[135]

As previously mentioned, when Diarmuid O'Leary was taken into the R.I.C. barracks in Midleton for possible identification, he gave a false name. His mother and sister were convinced he was lying dead somewhere. They went as far as purchasing a burial plot for him and holding a wake. Eventually, he wrote to his mother telling her he was a prisoner.[136]

A closer inspection of the official R.I.C. report of the battle, illustrates the overall effectiveness of the I.R.A. campaign in neutralising this once efficient force, despite their defeat at Clonmult. Two weeks after the battle, the R.I.C. still had not corrected the number of I.R.A. men killed, and more noticeable is the fact that they did not have the correct name of their most wanted man in east Cork, Diarmuid O'Hurley.

The leader of the rebel gang – Jeremiah Hurley – who had been operating in this District for a considerable time is believed to have been killed in this attack, but the body was taken away during the night. It was the only body removed.[137]

The five wounded prisoners of the battle spent some time in the Military Hospital, in Victoria Barracks, before being lodged in the Military Detention Barracks to join their three unwounded colleagues. Seven of the eight men did not have long to wait for their courts-martial. Due to the wound to his mouth, Paddy Higgins was not tried alongside his comrades. However, his turn would come later, on the 21st of June.

Courts-martial

On the 1st of March, 1921, a summary of the evidence against the seven captured I.R.A. volunteers was taken in Victoria Barracks, Cork. The Field General Court-Martial of the accused began in the gymnasium of Victoria Barracks, on Tuesday, the 8th of March.[138] The court-martial officials consisted of, three British Army officers adjudicating, there was no requirement for any of these officers to be legally trained, but the most senior had to hold the substantive rank of captain.[139] A British Army Judge-Advocate was present, to provide legal advice to the prosecutors and a prosecutor for the Crown. A death sentence required the unanimous verdict of all three judges, it could not be carried out, however, until it could be confirmed by the Commander-in-Chief.[140] The accused, Patrick O'Sullivan, Maurice Moore, Diarmuid O'Leary, John Harty, William Garde, Edmund Terry and Robert Walsh, were charged:

> With committing an offence in that they, at Clonmult, in the County Cork, on the 20th day of February, 1921, did, with other persons unknown, levy war against His Majesty by attacking with arms a detachment of His Majesty's Forces.[141]

Mr. Michael Comyn, K.C., (instructed by Mr. C.K. Murphy, solicitor) appeared for William Garde, Robert Walsh, Edmund Terry and John Harty. Mr. Joseph McCarthy, B.L., (instructed by Mr. Maurice O'Connor, solicitor), represented Maurice Moore, Patrick O'Sullivan and Diarmuid O'Leary.

The accused men pleaded not guilty. In opening the case, the Prosecutor produced a proclamation, issued by the Military Governor, prescribing the County of Cork as a Martial Law area, and pointing out that persons convicted of certain offences, were liable to suffer the penalty of death.[142]

The details of the events that occurred at Clonmult on the day of the battle were presented by the prosecution. After this, evidence was tendered by the military doctor, who was on duty in the Military Hospital. He stated that five wounded prisoners were brought in, suffering from gunshot wounds. Next, one of the officers, unnamed, who was present during the battle, gave his evidence. He gave details of the deployment of the troops after they left the vehicles at Rathorgan crossroads and the encirclement of the house. He witnessed the initial engagement resulting in the deaths of Michael Desmond and John Joe Joyce and also the breakout attempted by Jack O'Connell's party. He confirmed that Auxiliary Police reinforcements arrived from Midleton, the setting fire to the roof of the building and the subsequent surrender. He stated that there were shots fired from the building immediately after the first group of I.R.A. men emerged and that these men were shot while attempting to escape.[143]

The next witness, who was also an unnamed British Army officer, gave similar evidence, with the additional information that approximately twenty Auxiliary Police reinforcements arrived from Midleton.[144] Evidence was taken from three soldiers who were present, one had been detailed to fire on the only window at the rear of the house. Another was one of the soldiers who had travelled to Midleton for reinforcements. The third witness stated that the surrender happened approximately fifteen minutes after the roof had been set on fire.[145]

Another unnamed British Army officer was the next witness for the prosecution. He stated that it was he who set fire to the roof and also that none of the troops present were under his command.[146] This leads me to conclude that he was, Lieut. H. Hammond, M.C., who was intelligence officer of the 17th Infantry Brigade and was an officer of the Dorsetshire Regiment. Another British Army officer to give evidence had been positioned at the front of the house with Company Sergeant Major Edward Corney and a Private soldier, when Jack O'Connell emerged from the house. Shots were exchanged between the three soldiers and Jack O'Connell, during which C.S.M. Corney was wounded in the shoulder.[147] One of the army officers previously examined was recalled. He had made out a list of arms and ammunition found at the farmhouse. There were 13 rifles and carbines, 12 revolvers, 198 rounds of service ammunition, a Mills bomb, 2 shot-guns, bayonets and equipment.[148]

Opening the case for the defence, one of the accused, Edmund Terry, stated that he was wounded in the wrist and stomach, he was 17 years of age and came from Churchtown [South]. He further stated that he was not a member of Sinn Féin, Irish Volunteers, Fianna, nor of the I.R.A. His evidence was that he went to 9.30 a.m. mass on that Sunday, in Churchtown South with his mother. After mass, he met John Harty and decided that they would go to Clonmult that afternoon, to visit his grandmother. After their dinner, they set off for Clonmult and on the way they met Robert Walsh and William Garde at Ladysbridge. From there the four cycled to Clonmult, arriving there at around 2.30 p.m. Edmund Terry went to his grandmother's house, which was at the crossroads in the village. Meanwhile, the other three waited outside the door where they met Dick Hegarty, who eventually brought the four of them to the farmhouse. They were at the farmhouse about ten minutes when someone shouted at them to come inside, immediately after this the shooting started. He spent the duration of the battle on the floor of the farmhouse. He emerged from the house after the surrender and it was at this stage he received the three gunshot wounds, two in the stomach and one in the wrist.[149] He spent three days in hospital.[150]

The first witness on Tuesday, 15th of March, was the mother of Edmund Terry, who corroborated the evidence given by her son, and added that she had given him money to purchase cigarettes for his grandmother. The next witness was a young girl who stated that Edmund Terry and John Harty had purchased either two or three packets of cigarettes in Churchtown South, on that Sunday morning.

The next examined was the defendant John Harty whose evidence concurred with that of Edmund Terry, he also stated that, 'after the surrender he was about 25 yards outside the door when he was hit on the side of the head by something, he thought it was the butt end of a rifle.' He spent three days in hospital and also denied that he was a member of any illegal organisation.[151]

William Garde was the next defendant to be examined. He denied being a member of any illegal organisation and also stated that he met his first cousin, Robert Walsh, at Ballycotton mass. Afterwards, they had dinner together in Garde's house and then decided to go for a cycle. They met Edmund Terry and John Harty in Ladysbridge and agreed to go with them to Clonmult.[152] The main part of his evidence was the same as that given by the previous defendants. Detailing the events following his surrender he stated that, 'the shot was fired just after they came out into the yard. That was the shot that felled the man in front of him. The second shot hit the witness in the forearm'.[153]

William Garde's father was the first in the witness box on Wednesday, 16th of March where he confirmed the evidence given by his wife. The accused Robert Walsh was next to be examined. His evidence of the events of that Sunday morning mirrored that of William Garde. The witness stated that he had joined the Royal Munster Fusiliers during the Great War, but had been discharged as he was under age. He next joined the Leinster Regiment and was transferred to the Royal Irish [Regiment], but was discharged for the same reason. His evidence for the events at Clonmult was the same as given by the previous defendants.[154] Robert Walsh's mother was examined next and she provided a character witness for her son. A letter was produced by Mr. Comyn, from an R.I.C. sergeant 'in which Walsh and Garde were given excellent characters.' This closed the evidence in the cases of the accused for which Mr. Comyn appeared.

Mr. McCarthy, B.L., speaking on behalf of Maurice Moore, Patrick O'Sullivan and Diarmuid O'Leary, opened with a character reference for O'Sullivan. He stated that two of Patrick

O'Sullivan's brothers fought in the Great War and one of them had been killed. Patrick O'Sullivan gave evidence that he himself was on the run from the I.R.A. and was in fact a prisoner at Clonmult. He admitted to being a member of Sinn Féin but that he was not a Volunteer. He admitted being the acting secretary of the Sinn Féin Arbitration Court in Queenstown. After the court was raided by the military, he stated he had to go on the run from the I.R.A. because it was believed that he had given the details of the court to the military. His story was that he was arrested in a public house in Clonmult on the Friday prior to the battle and was brought to the farmhouse as a prisoner.[155]

Patrick O'Sullivan was cross examined by the Prosecutor and in his defence he swore that he was not a section commander of the I.R.A. He was questioned about his position in the Arbitration Court and was also questioned as to why he was able to work so close to home, while claiming to be on the run from the I.R.A.

Maurice Moore was next to be examined. He stated that he was at home in Queenstown on the morning of the battle, when he decided to cycle to Carrigtwohill and on to Midleton. He met James Aherne in Midleton and Aherne told him that Patrick O'Sullivan was a prisoner in Clonmult, and that he was to go out to identify him. The two men were at the farmhouse solely for the purpose of identifying O'Sullivan, when the British troops arrived there and as a result they were trapped inside. After the surrender, he was taken by one of the British officers to identify some of the bodies. He identified Jeremiah Aherne, James Glavin and David Desmond.[156] He admitted to being a member of the I.R.A., Sinn Féin and the Fianna but swore he was not a member of the militant wing of any of them. His father was next to be examined and stated that his son was at home on that Sunday morning.

The evidence produced by Diarmuid O'Leary was that he was the only surviving son of his widowed mother. Two of his brothers had died at home from injuries received in the Great War; he had one sister. He impersonated Dick Hegarty and gave evidence that he was in Ballymacoda on the Sunday morning. There he met a girl whom he knew, who asked him to take a parcel to Clonmult, to a man whose name was Hegarty. He was directed to the farmhouse, where he gave the parcel to Dick Hegarty. He just happened to be in the house when the military arrived, therefore, he too was trapped inside. He threw himself on top of a bed, and after three or four shots were fired, a dog jumped on top of him. 'Raising himself, being afraid that the dog would bite him, he was wounded in the head.'[157] He stated that he was not a member of Sinn Féin, the Irish Volunteers or the I.R.A.

The young girl, who was mentioned by Diarmuid O'Leary, was examined next and swore that she gave the parcel of clothes for Dick Hegarty to O'Leary, in Ballymacoda, on the Sunday morning. A youth was questioned who supported this evidence by swearing that he met O'Leary, in Mogeely, on the Sunday and that O'Leary told him that he was on his way to Clonmult.

On Saturday, 19th of March, the trial concluded with the closing addresses given by Mr. Comyn and Mr. McCarthy. On behalf of the men they represented, both Comyn and McCarthy reaffirmed their belief in the innocence of the accused of the charges against them.

The evidence given by the four accused, Harty, Garde, Walsh and Terry was only partially accurate. It is quite understandable that they did not volunteer that the cigarettes that Garde bought were for the members of the column and not for his grandmother. The principal reason for the four going to Clonmult was to deliver money which had been collected from the farmers in their area for the I.R.A. As well as being the column headquarters, it was a collecting point for these funds. The evidence given by the three accused, O'Sullivan, Moore and O'Leary could not have been further from the truth. They were all active I.R.A. men who were fully involved in the column.

During the course of the court-martial, the legal team for the accused made an attempt to halt the proceedings on a number of legal issues. These issues formed the basis for an appeal to a higher civil court in Dublin in the aftermath of the trial. On the Tuesday following the court-martial, it was announced that three of the prisoners, Patrick O'Sullivan, Maurice Moore and Diarmuid O'Leary were to be executed. The fate of the other four was not immediately made known. An appeal was immediately lodged and a temporary order was granted by the King's Bench Division of the High Court in Dublin on the 23rd of March. This prevented the Military authorities in Cork from carrying out the death sentences imposed on three of the seven I.R.A. men, pending a full appeal being heard.

Letters were sent by the members of Midleton U.D.C. to the Prime Minister in Downing St., and to the Chief Secretary's Office in Dublin, appealing for the lives of the three men.

The appeal was heard in Dublin on the 20th and 21st of April, 1921 and was listed as "The King (Garde and Others) v. MAJOR-GENERAL E. P. STRICKLAND and Others.[158] The appeal was heard before Moloney C.J. and Dodd, Pim, Gordon and Samuels J.J. The order was applied for on the grounds:[159]

1. That the Military Court had no jurisdiction to try the prisoners.
2. That no state of war existed sufficiently to justify the existence of martial law or a Court established in pursuance thereof.
3. That the names, professions, and places of abode of the witnesses for the prosecution were not given according to law or at all.
4. That the names of the members of the Military Court were not given.
5. That the said William Garde, John Harty, Edmund Terry, Maurice Moore, Robert Walsh, Pat Sullivan, and Diarmuid O'Leary were indicted and tried without the oath of two lawful witnesses to an overt act of treason.

The appeal hinged on whether or not a state of war existed in Cork. If a state of war did exist, then the authorities were deemed as correct in declaring the region as a martial law area and consequently, persons captured under arms could be tried by military court-martial.

Affidavits were presented from prominent citizens of Cork, declaring that 'normal life, entertainment and business life of the city and county daily continued and that the courts were still sitting.' In reply, an affidavit was sworn by General Macready that 'a state of open rebellion existed, amounting to actual warfare of a guerrilla character, and that ordinary life was carried on due to the presence of large numbers of crown forces.'[160] General Macready also listed the casualty figures for the crown forces in the martial law areas to prove his submission that a state of war did exist.[161] Precedence had been set in a previous appeal, Rex v. Allen, February 1921, where it was conceded that a state of war did exist.[162] The appeal finished on the 21st of April, and the judgement was delivered to the Court by the Lord Chief Justice on the 25th.[163]

The Lord Chief Justice briefly recounted the events that led to the court-martial, the background to the introduction of Martial Law and the grounds on which the appeal was made. He went on:

> In the case of The King v. Allen in which I delivered the judgement of the Court on the 24th of February last, we were unanimously of the opinion that there was at that date a state of war in the area included in the Lord Lieutenant's proclamation justifying the application of martial law, and the only question which arises for decision in the present case is as to whether that state of war still continues.[164]

The affidavit sworn by Gen. Macready highlighting the crown forces casualties in the Martial Law area, was sufficient to convince the appeal judges that the state of war did indeed still exist.

The Lord Chief Justice concluded the judgement:

The attempt to distinguish this case from Allen's Case therefore fails on all grounds, and we must discharge the conditional order.[165]

Having failed in the legal appeal, the local representatives in Cork city and in east Cork opened a petition on the 26th, which was signed by the families, friends and supporters of the three condemned men. The petition books were available in the city, the Town Halls in Midleton and Cobh and in the Carnegie Library in Killeagh.[166] The petitions were to be sent to the Lord Lieutenant in Dublin. This was the last chance to save the lives of the three I.R.A. men. The lives of Patrick O'Sullivan, Maurice Moore and Diarmuid O'Leary, were hanging by a thread.

The executions

The eight weeks between 28th of January and the 23rd of March 1921, were particularly costly in terms of lives lost for the I.R.A. in county Cork:

- At Dripsey, an I.R.A. ambushing party was taken by surprise by British troops, when the location of the ambush was reported to the authorities by a local Loyalist, Mrs. Mary Lindsay. Six I.R.A. men and two civilians were taken prisoner. One of the I.R.A., men later died of his wounds. The seven others were subsequently court-martialled and two were executed.[167]
- On the 15th of February, at Mourne Abbey, south of Mallow, in Liam Lynch's Second Brigade area, an ambushing party was also taken by surprise. In the battle, four of the I.R.A. men died and eight were taken prisoner, of whom two were later executed.[168]
- On the same day, in the Third Brigade area, three I.R.A. men and six civilians were killed, during a failed ambush at Upton railway station.[169]

- Two days later, the Thursday before Clonmult, in west Cork, four I.R.A. men were taken by surprise and killed, while cutting a trench across a road near Kilbrittain five miles south of Bandon.

- The following Sunday, the Battle of Clonmult took place, resulting in twelve dead and eight prisoners taken.

- On the 23rd of March, seven I.R.A. men were asleep in a shed at Clogheen on the outskirts of Cork city, without sentries on guard. Their location was passed onto the British, who immediately raided the building. Six men were shot dead.[170]

A factor common to five of the six above reversals, was the lack of advance warning. The importance of sentries was still not fully appreciated. Following the engagements at Dripsey, Mourne Abbey and Clonmult, the British had a total of twenty-four prisoners. The men were tried by Field General Court Martial in Victoria Barracks, Cork as they were captured in the Martial Law area. The trials were held in the gymnasium in the barracks.

In the aftermath of these three reversals, the I.R.A. did not immediately seek revenge for their losses. However, on the 17th of February, following the Dripsey ambush, the I.R.A. kidnapped Mrs. Mary Lindsay and her chauffeur, James Clarke, because she had informed the British of the ambush.[171] When, following their courts-martial, five of the I.R.A. men were sentenced to be executed the authorities were told by the I.R.A., that the hostages would only be released in exchange for the lives of the I.R.A. men. The five from Dripsey and a sixth from Tipperary, were executed in the Military Detention Block of Victoria Barracks, on the 28th of February and the two hostages were shot shortly afterwards.

On the night of the executions, the Officer Commanding First Brigade I.R.A., Sean O'Hegarty, unleashed his men. Between 6.30 p.m. and 8.00 p.m. gunfire was heard all over the city. The result was that the Active Service Unit in Cork city under Pa Murray, shot dead six British soldiers and a further four were wounded.[172] This was the pattern established in the aftermath of Clonmult: no immediate reprisals, attempt to take a prominent person hostage and unleash the gunmen, only if all else fails.

Following the courts-martial of the Clonmult and Mourne Abbey prisoners, an instruction was issued by I.R.A Brigade headquarters in Cork, to attempt to kidnap a senior British Army officer. Shortly afterwards, the I.R.A. men under Frank Busteed, kidnapped Major G. L. Compton-Smith of the Royal Welch Fusiliers, who was the officer in charge of Ballyvonaire Camp, located between Buttevant and Mallow.[173] He had travelled alone on the train from Buttevant on the 16th of April, and had left the train at Blarney to walk the short distance to Smith's hotel in the village.[174] A dispatch was sent to Gen. Strickland, informing him that Major Compton-Smith was a prisoner of the I.R.A. and was being held in exchange for the lives of the men who were under sentence of death, following Clonmult and Mourne Abbey.[175] He was held in safe houses in the vicinity of Donoughmore, in mid-Cork. During his time in captivity, he was allowed write to his wife Gladys in England. Despite widespread searches by the British forces in the area, he remained in I.R.A. hands.

In the weeks between the Battle of Clonmult and the executions of Patrick O'Sullivan and Maurice Moore, there were very few incidents in the 4th Battalion area. This was primarily because most of the men who had been active were either dead or captured. However, on Sunday 10th of April, Diarmuid O'Hurley, Joseph Aherne, Paddy Whelan, and other activists attempted to blow up a British Army convoy as it passed Ballyedikin junction, three miles east of Midleton, on the road to Youghal.[176] They placed a bomb against the front wall of the court house in the early hours of the following morning, causing considerable damage.

The day before the executions, Diarmuid O'Leary was in the exercise yard of the Military Detention Barracks with Patrick O'Sullivan and Maurice Moore, when he was called for a visit.

His mother and sister were waiting to see him. When the visit was over, he went back to the exercise yard to find that his two comrades had been removed to their cells. During the interim, orders had been received by the prison authorities that the two men were to be executed the following morning. The condemned men, two from Clonmult and two from Mourne Abbey, were thus confined to their cells until the following morning. A black cross was pinned to their cell doors and sentries were placed outside their cells.

The transcript of Vol. Patrick O'Sullivan's last letter to his mother, written in Cork Military Detention Barracks on the eve of his execution.[177]

MILITARY BARRACKS, CORK.

27th of April, 1921.

MY DEAREST MOTHER,

I sincerely hope and trust that God and His Blessed Virgin Mother Mary will comfort and console you and enable yourself and poor father to bear this trial with patience and to suffer all for the holy Will of God; also my loving brothers, relations and friends.

I am in great spirits and pray for the hour to come when I will be released from this world of sorrow and suffering. We must all die some day, and I am simply going by an early train. Jesus and Mary were my friends and supports in all the trials of life, and now that death is coming they are truer and better friends than ever.

You can rest assured that I will be happy in Heaven, and although I have to leave you in mourning, you will be consoled to think that I am going to meet God in Heaven and also my brothers and sister. Why should I fear to die, when death will only unite me to God in Heaven. If I could choose my own death, I would not ask to die otherwise. In fact I am delighted to have had such a glorious opportunity of gaining eternal salvation as well as serving my country. My death will help with the others, and remember that those who die for Ireland never die.

Don't let my death cause you too much unnecessary worry or grief, and then when I get to Heaven I will constantly pray to God for the kind and loving parents He gave me, to help them to bear this little Cross. Tell my loving brothers and friends that I will also remember them.

Good-bye now, my dearest and best of mothers, until we meet again in Heaven and God.

Your fond and loving son,

Paddy.

That night, Diarmuid O'Leary received a visit from a priest who told him he was to be shot in the morning. Later a soldier who brought him tea, told him, 'they are keeping you for your mate in hospital.' O'Leary recalled, 'Apparently we were to be shot in pairs. I need scarcely say I did not have much sleep that night.'[178]

On Thursday, 28th of April, 1921, four men were executed in the Military Detention Barracks in Cork, now Cork Prison. Thomas Mulcahy (18) and Patrick Ronayne (24) were executed having being captured at Mourne Abbey; Patrick O'Sullivan (22) and Maurice Moore (24), both of Cobh, for their involvement at Clonmult. The men received their last visitors on the previous day.

The executions were carried out yesterday morning [at 8.00 and 8.15]. Very Rev. Canon O'Sullivan and Rev. W. O'Brien, C.C. were with the prisoners at an early hour in the morning. At 7 o' clock they assisted at mass celebrated by Father O'Brien and received Holy Communion. At 7.30 a.m., Canon O'Sullivan said Mass and the prisoners were joined in their prayers by Rev. Father O'Brien.[179]

After the Masses in the oratory, the prisoners were removed to their cells, and within a few minutes, accompanied by the Rev. Canon O'Sullivan and Fr. O'Brien, were marched to the place of execution in pairs. When the firing party discharged the volley they withdrew and the priests then went to the dead men and anointed them and imparted Papal Benediction. The prisoners met their death with firmness and fortitude.[180]

Following the executions, the four bodies were transported by military ambulance to the Cork city jail, off Western Road. The bodies were buried beside their comrades who had been executed for Dripsey. Applications made by their families to the military authorities for the return of the bodies, were refused. The bodies remain buried there to this day.

On the morning of the executions, at 11 o'clock in St. Colman's Cathedral in Cobh, a Solemn Requiem Mass was said for the repose of the souls of the two natives of that town. The mass was celebrated by Rev. D. O'Keeffe. All the shops in the town were closed. At Rushbrook Convent Chapel, early morning mass was celebrated by Rev. P. Fouhy for the same intention.[181]

On the evening of the executions, Diarmuid O'Leary was taken to an office in the barracks, where three British Army officers were present. He recalled, 'One of them proceeded to read out the sentence of death passed on me and then added that the sentence was commuted to one of penal servitude for life. It is not possible to state the relief I felt at this totally unexpected news.'[182]

On Friday, the 29th, it was officially announced that the five remaining prisoners that had been court-martialled, had been reprieved.[183]

Paddy Higgins was still awaiting his court-martial which eventually opened in Victoria Barracks on Monday, 21st of June.

The I.R.A. and Crown Forces reprisals

On the 29th of April, the day after the executions, Major Compton-Smith was informed by an unnamed I.R.A. Brigade officer, who was accompanied by the C.O. of the 6th Battalion, Jackie O'Leary, that he was to be shot. He was given one hour to prepare for his execution. He made two last requests. Firstly, he wished to write a last letter to his wife and secondly he requested 'the benefit of spiritual consolation from a clergyman' before he died. His first request was granted, but, as there was no Protestant clergyman in the vicinity of Donoughmore, his second request was refused.[184] Before entering the shed where Major Compton-Smith was held captive, Jackie O'Leary gave instructions to a few men about digging a grave. Inside he gave pen and paper to the prisoner who wrote:

> I am to be shot in an hour's time. Dearest, your hubby will die with your name on his lips, your face before my eyes, and he will die like an Englishman and a soldier. I cannot tell you, sweetheart, how much it means to me to leave you alone. I have only the dearest, tenderest, love for you and my sweet little daughter, Annie. I leave my cigarette case to my regiment, my miniature medals to my father, and my watch to the officer who is about to execute me, because I believe him to be a gentleman and to mark the fact that I bear no malice for carrying out what he sincerely believes to be his duty.
>
> Tender, tender farewell and kisses; Your Own, "Jack".[185]

Before he was led out, he requested some warm water to 'wash my body before I return it to the Lord' afterwards he prayed as he was led across two fields:[186]

> "Now the labourer' task is o'er,
> Now the battle day is past,
> Now upon the farther shore,
> Lands the voyager at last".

At the end of the field was a freshly dug grave. He turned to look at the grave and following a short prayer he faced the firing squad. Jackie O' Leary gave the orders, "Aim at the target". Before he ordered "Fire", Compton-Smith was heard to say "I love you Gladys.[187]

Major Compton-Smith's body remained in that grave until handed over to the Gardaí in late 1924. He was re-interred in Fort Davis, Whitegate in 1925.

After the executions, the I.R.A. were bent on revenge. After Clonmult every suspected informer and every man in uniform (including coastguards and marines) became a legitimate target to be 'shot on sight' in the I.R.A.'s quest for vengeance.[188]

On Saturday night, 30th of April, ex-soldier, Michael O'Keeffe was the target of an I.R.A. snatch squad in the village of Carrigtwohill. The following morning, his body was found with an I.R.A. label attached, declaring him a convicted spy. The body was removed to his home. To quote the C.O. of the 4th Battalion, Mick Leahy:

> I sent Dathaí O'Brien to pick up [Michael] O'Keeffe[189] there [in Carrigtwohill] for we had the goods on him. I told him to go down and get this man. O'Brien arrived back in an old Ford car… 'He's in Patsy Connors' he said. 'But I told you to bring him back here'. 'I know that' O'Brien said, 'He's on the sidewalk outside and we couldn't bring him back because he's dead. We went down to his house and when we were passing up the street at Patsy Connors' I turned round and let him have it for he jumped out of the car'.[190]

The killings continued the following day, Sunday, 1st of May, when two Black and Tans were attacked by armed and masked men in a wood beside the village of Castlemartyr, six miles east of Midleton.[191] Constable William Albert Smith was shot dead and Constable John F. Webb later died of his wounds. The official reprisals followed swiftly. The licensed premises of Mrs. Ellen

Cronin, and the house of Michael Fitzgerald, both in the village of Clonmult, were destroyed on the 6th of May. The furniture and personal effects of Patrick Hegarty and William O'Connell, both residents of Castlemartyr were also destroyed on the same day.

These destructions were ordered by Colonel Commandant H. W. Higginson, C.B., D.S.O., Commanding 17th Infantry Brigade and Military Governor, on the grounds that their owners were supporters of the armed rebels, and that such armed rebels carried out a murderous attack on two members of the R.I.C. at Castlemartyr on 1st of May, 1921.[192] The burning of the two buildings in Clonmult have often been regarded as direct reprisals for the Battle of Clonmult. However, I have now discovered that they were indirect reprisals for the killing of the two Black and Tans. These were in turn killed as reprisals for the execution of the two I.R.A. men captured for Clonmult. Before this research, it was widely believed that the burnings were carried out as reprisals for the support of the column in Clonmult.

At about 2.30 a.m. on Sunday, 8th of May, three volunteers, William Bransfield, Jack Hayes and Dick Masterson who worked in Keegan's, were dragged from their homes in Carrigtwohill by a party of disguised Crown forces. Hayes and Keegan managed to escape but Vol. William Bransfield, was shot dead. He was about twenty-five years old and had been employed by the Great Southern and Western Railway Company.[193] He was buried in the Republican Plot in Midleton, alongside the Clonmult men.

On Saturday, the 14th of May, 1921, the Crown Forces in Midleton suffered their bloodiest day of the War of Independence. At about 3.00 p.m., R.I.C. Sergeant Joseph Coleman was having a drink in Buckley's public house and grocer's premises on the Main Street, when he was shot dead by a local I.R.A man. When four policemen arrived on the scene, two of them were sent to get a doctor and a priest to minister to the dying sergeant. They were ambushed at the southern end of the town and the two Black and Tans, Thomas Cornyn from Cavan and Harold Thompson, an Australian, were killed.[194] The I.R.A. attacked a second party of police who were sent to the scene and during this engagement a Constable Mc Donald was wounded.[195] The I.R.A. placed a note on the dead body of Constable Thompson, which read simply, 'revenge for Clonmult etc.' The Midleton I.R.A. were convinced that Constable Thompson had been present at Clonmult and local folklore has since exaggerated this note to:

> Revenge for Clonmult we'll have some more,
> You drove to Clonmult, you'll drive no more.

Also on the same day, two unnamed gunners from the Royal Marine Artillery, stationed in the Coastguard Station at East Ferry, were drinking in a public house in Ballinacurra, just outside Midleton.[196] That evening while walking back to their station, they were abducted just outside Ballinacurra, in the town-land of Loughcarrig. The two young Marines had grass stuffed into their mouths before being shot dead. Their bodies were thrown into a local quarry.

During the early hours of the following day, 15th of May, Michael Aherne (brother of Volunteer Jack Aherne), Ballyrichard, Midleton, Richard Barry, Knockgrifin, Midleton and John Ryan, Woodstock, Carrigtwohill, were taken from their homes by British soldiers from the Cameron Highlanders Regiment. Their bullet-riddled bodies were found the following morning.[197] Two other men from Carrigtwohill, Richard Flynn and his son Timothy, were also taken by the military. Richard Flynn was found shot dead the following morning and his son, who was deaf and unable to speak, was seriously wounded.[198]

It is an indisputable fact that the British Army mobile patrol that travelled to Clonmult on the 20th of February, 1921, was acting on information received from an informer. The patrol travelled from Midleton to Clonmult using the most covert route, they stopped at Rathorgan crossroads and deployed immediately for the farmhouse. The local civilians who went to the crossroads were arrested and warned not to go near one of the tenders. The informer was hidden onboard.

Following the battle the I.R.A. were determined to locate the informer. They believed that the culprit was an ex-serviceman who had been seen trapping rabbits in the area. In the aftermath of Clonmult at least two Irishmen, who had served in the British forces, were killed in Carrigtwohill by the I.R.A. Michael O'Keeffe an ex-soldier, was shot on Saturday, 30th of April and Daniel O'Callaghan, an ex-sailor was killed on Tuesday, 21st of June.

During May, the I.R.A. in the Watergrasshill–Glenville vicinity, which was in the 'C' Company, 1st Battalion, 2nd Brigade area, arrested David Walsh an ex-soldier, whom they were convinced was the informer.[199] He was questioned by the officer commanding the Company, who attempted to get a confession from him, initially without success. He was taken to a freshly dug grave where he was told he would be shot if he did not confess. He was also told that if he did confess he would be exiled to Australia. He eventually made a confession and based on this he was court-martialled. Found guilty of informing on the column at Clonmult, he was duly shot. On the 21st of May, the adjutant of the 1st Battalion sent a report on the arrest, interrogation and execution of David Walsh to the commanding officer of the 4th Battalion.[200]

Letter detailing the capture and execution of David Walsh

The following is a transcript of the letter sent to the O.C. 4th Battalion detailing the arrest and subsequent execution of David Walsh:[201]

"A" Headquarters
Cork No 2 Brigade
21. 5. 21

To the O/C 4th Battalion
Cork No 1. Brigade

1. Yours to hand on 20th inst.

2. The following will be of interest to you. The report re this spy has been filed away, so what I am writing is from memory.

3. Our C. Coy Capt. arrested a suspicious person of the tramp class, and detained him on suspicion for two days.[202] During this time he could get no information from him beyond the fact that he was David Walsh of Shanagarry, and that he was looking for work in Glenville. To extract information from him, the Capt. brought him the local C.C. one evening and next morning had a grave made away on the mountains. Here he brought the prisoner, and informed him he was to be shot, and the only way he had of saving his life was by giving full information re himself and his accomplices. If this was forthcoming the Capt. guaranteed him a free pass to Australia. The prisoner then disclosed to the Capt. how he had seen your men at Clonmult and meeting a military party on his way to Cork, he informed a military officer, and that he himself led the party down to your camp. For this he received a lump sum and was taken on as a permanent paid spy at £1 per week and the promise of a lump sum for any good catch made on his information. He then gave the names of those already forwarded to you as paid spies.

4. David Walsh was subsequently tried by court-martial for espionage and found guilty and sentenced to be shot. The finding was confirmed by our Batt. O/C and the sentence was duly executed.

Signed
Adjutant

The I.R.A. concluded that Walsh had been trapping rabbits near Clonmult and had spotted some of the volunteers returning from confessions in Dungourney, on the Saturday evening prior to the battle. He was making his way to Cork on the Sunday morning when he stopped the British Army patrol. He then guided them to Clonmult.

The British account of the killing of David Walsh is as follows.[203] Some idea of the method of extracting information by threats of violence is demonstrated in the case of a man named David Walsh, a detailed account of whose treatment was found in a captured document. He was arrested by the I.R.A., for being 'a suspicious person of the tramp class' and he was detained for two days, during which time no information could be obtained from him. In order to remedy this, he was removed to a lonely mountain, and was confronted with the parish priest and an empty grave, and informed that he was to be shot forthwith, unless he supplied them with full information concerning himself and his accomplices. If this was forthcoming, the Captain guaranteed him a free pass to Australia. The unfortunate man, with the prospect of imminent death staring him in the face, invented a story of having met a military party on the way to Cork, and having given them information concerning a camp at Clonmult. The way in which the I.R.A. captain fulfilled his guarantee is told in the final paragraph of the document, which reads, 'David Walsh was subsequently tried by court-martial for espionage, found guilty and sentenced to be shot. The finding was duly confirmed and the sentence duly executed.'[204]

On the morning of 28th of May, 1921, Commandant Diarmuid O'Hurley set off alone and on foot, armed with a revolver and a grenade, from Jack Ring's house at Ballyriorta, on the north-eastern side of Midleton.[205] The Cameron Highlanders were constantly raiding Carrigtwohill from their base in Cobh and the local volunteers were doing nothing about it. Commandant O'Hurley was going to meet Carrigtwohill I.R.A. officers to admonish them for their lack of activity on the matter. He travelled around the north side of Midleton using byroads. He was crossing the road beside the old graveyard at Gurtacrue, when he was surprised by a joint R.I.C./Army bicycle patrol. He attempted to run from the scene but he was shot down and mortally wounded. The British did not learn who they had killed until the following day. By then, Commandant O'Hurley's body had been taken to Paddy Daly's house at Gurteen, just across the fields from the site of the Battle of Clonmult.[206] From there, his body was taken to Ballintotis Church and on the following day he was buried temporarily in Churchtown North cemetery. During the Truce he was re-interred adjacent to the Republican Plot of Holy Rosary Cemetery, Midleton, beside his comrades.[207]

Three days later, on the 31st of May, the I.R.A. detonated the bomb primed by Paddy Whelan at Clonmult, beside the band of the Hampshire Regiment. Two Youghal volunteers, Paddy O'Reilly and Thomas Power detonated the device; Paddy was the trigger man.[208] The band was leading a Company of the Regiment, from the town towards the shooting range at Youghal for Lewis Gun practice:

> When the clouds of dust settled, some twenty men and boys were seen lying on the ground, and pitiful groans and cries for help were heard. Two corporals, two bandsmen and two boys were killed and nineteen of the band wounded.[209]

The Truce was declared at noon on Monday, 11th of July, 1921 the same day, the mother of the two Clonmult boys, Michael and David Desmond, passed away.

There was further tragedy for the Hampshires before they left Ireland. In Macroom, on the 22nd of April, 1922, Lieut. G.R.A. Dove, who had been present at Clonmult on the day of the battle, was travelling to Killarney, along with two other officers from other regiments and their driver, when they were kidnapped by the I.R.A. Their four bodies were found at Kilgobnait, west of Macroom, approximately eighteen months later.[210]

The Court-martial of Capt. Paddy Higgins

Capt. Paddy Higgins was the eighth and last of the Clonmult prisoners to be court-martialled. He had been injured following the surrender and after recovering from the wound to his mouth, he was found to be suffering from appendicitis. He was eventually declared fit and released from the barracks hospital on the 28th of April.[211] His court-martial proceedings began on the Friday, 17th of June, 1921, when he was served with his charge sheet in his cell in the Military Detention Barracks in Cork.[212]

Paddy Higgins was charged with committing an offence: 'in that he, at Clonmult, County Cork, on the 20th of February 1921, with Jeremiah O' Leary and other persons, did levy war against his Majesty the King, by attacking a detachment of his Majesty's troops'.[213] His court-martial opened in Victoria Barracks, Cork, on Tuesday, 21st of June, 1921. The court consisted of three military officers acting as jurors with a fourth acting in the capacity of Judge Advocate.[214] He was defended by Mr. George Daly, B.L., instructed by Mr. William J. Barry, solicitor, Midleton.[215] It was noticed by the defence legal team that one of the British officers adjudicating, had been involved in the first Clonmult trial. After a legal argument, this officer was replaced. When the trial recommenced, the accused pleaded not guilty.

The case for the prosecution followed on the very same lines as with his comrades. Evidence was taken from some of the Auxiliary Police, British soldiers and officers who were present at Clonmult. Evidence was given identifying Paddy Higgins as being present and of being captured after the battle and it was also stated that he had not attempted to escape following his surrender. A Royal Army Medical Corps corporal also identified the accused as one of the prisoners brought to the hospital of Cork Barracks, following the battle.[216]

The accused was examined on the first day of the trial. He stated that he was twenty-three years old and resided with his parents at Ardra, Rostellan, Co. Cork. His defence rested upon the claim that he could not have been a member of the I.R.A., due to his delicate physical condition. This stemmed from eight years previously when, as a pupil at St. Colman's College, Fermoy, he was diagnosed with appendicitis. The operation was not fully successful and he had an ongoing problem with his appendix. As with his comrades during the first Clonmult trial, Paddy Higgins gave a generally false account of his activities in the weeks leading up to the battle. He stated that, during November 1920, the military had raided his home and this had frightened his mother to such an extent that she had pleaded with him to go on the run. He moved to a motor firm in Clonmel, County Tipperary but he had returned home on the 14th of February when his appendix became inflamed again. He moved to a relative's house near Conna, and on Saturday, 19th of February, the day before the battle, he stated that he went to Midleton with his uncle where he met a school friend, Dick Hegarty, who took him to the farmhouse in Clonmult where he spent the night. He claimed not to have known any of the men he met in the farmhouse. He went to 8.30 a.m. mass the following day. He had his Sunday dinner in his sister's house and stated that the only reason he went back to the farmhouse was to retrieve some item he had left there. He was in the farmyard, pumping the tyre of his bicycle when the British troops arrived and that is how he came to be trapped in the house. He stated he had not seen arms in the house and had not taken any part in the attack.[217]

Cross examined by the prosecutor, the defendant stated that he was not a member of the I.R.A. He had been a member of the old Volunteers but had resigned due to his ill health.[218]

His mother was next to be called on for evidence. She stated that following the military raid on the 16th of November, she had advised her son to move in with his uncle. His uncle was called next and he confirmed that he had taken the accused to Midleton on the day before the battle and had seen him leave with a friend. A sister of the accused gave evidence of seeing her brother at mass with a friend on the morning of the battle. She also stated that Paddy had dinner in her house after mass and had returned to the farmhouse only because ha had left something behind. The second and last day of the trial was taken up with the summary of evidence. Following this the Judge Advocate reviewed the evidence and the court was closed.

Following the end of his court-martial on the 22nd of June, he was informed that night that he had been found guilty of the charges against him.[219] He was sentenced to be shot and that the sentence was subject to confirmation.[220] The following day his legal team immediately lodged an appeal with the Chancery Division in Dublin.

His appeal was heard in Dublin on Wednesday, 27th of June before the Master of the Rolls. Mr. H. Kennedy, K.C., Mr. Lynch, K.C. and Mr. John A. Costello (later Taoiseach), instructed by Mr. William Barry appeared on behalf of the plaintiff.

A writ was issued on his behalf claiming that the military court did not have the authority to try him, that military tribunals could only be set up by an Act of Parliament and that he was not subject to military law and that a state of war did not exist in the Martial Law area. The plaintiff also sought an interlocutory injunction, pending the hearing of his claim, for the declaration of right to enable him to have the question of constitutional right finally decided by the ultimate tribunal if necessary. This ultimate authority was the House of Lords. The plaintiff also sought relief by injunction, writ or habeas corpus or otherwise so as to prevent the defendants or any of them or any officer of the military or civil executive from imperilling the life and interfering with the liberty of the plaintiff.[221]

Following this, the appeal court heard the evidence that was presented at the court-martial. The point was made that there was grave reason to fear that the plaintiff was in imminent peril of his life, in that the sentence of death might be carried out at any moment and without any further notice unless the court intervened to prevent it. The Master of the Rolls granted a conditional order for a writ of habeas corpus directed to General Macready, General Strickland, and the Governor of the Detention Barracks, Cork.[222]

Before the findings of his first appeal were announced, his legal team made a fresh appeal on Tuesday, 19th of July. This appeal was heard, again by the Master of the Rolls, in the Chancery Division in Dublin. This appeal was for an order making absolute, the conditional order for a writ of habeas corpus, made by the Master of the Rolls, on the 27th of June.[223]

An issue that was raised during this appeal was why the prisoner was not tried before a formal Court-Martial rather than a Field General Court-Martial. The Crown's lawyers were unable to answer this point. The Master of the Rolls reserved judgement and directed that a telegram should be sent to the military, arresting the sentence passed on the plaintiff.[224]

This appeal was overshadowed by an appeal that was ongoing before the House of Lords in London, involving two Cork men under sentence of death having been captured in possession of fire-arms and ammunition. Patrick Clifford and Michael O'Sulllivan were arrested in April and following their trial were sentenced to death. The Irish Court of Appeal dismissed a subsequent appeal, holding that it was a criminal cause or matter, and that therefore, no appeal lay.[225] The case was then brought to the House of Lords where it opened on Thursday, 7th of July. The hearing was adjourned on Tuesday, 12th of July; the day after the Truce came into effect. The following Thursday it was announced that judgement was reserved in the appeal.[226] Events had overtaken circumstances, the guns had fallen silent since noon on the previous Monday, and the War of Independence was over. Paddy Higgins would not now be executed. The six surviving prisoners, captured at the Battle of Clonmult, remained in military custody and all were eventually released following the signing of the Treaty on the 6th of December, 1921.

Conclusion

For the Crown Forces the outcome of the Battle of Clonmult was a morale booster. It had combined good intelligence, the timely deployment of their forces to Clonmult, and effective tactics had been employed throughout the battle. It was one of the few occasions during the War of Independence in which they had wiped out a flying column.

I have concluded that the legal battles, fought by the I.R.A.'s legal representatives, both during the courts-martial and the subsequent appeals, should be judged as a partial success. The eight men captured were under threat of death, but the fact that just two were executed, was testament to the hard work of their legal teams. The legal battle, especially the appeals in Dublin, also had the effect of neutralising to some extent the powers of the military governors in the Martial Law area. The death penalties handed down by military courts-martial would have to be confirmed by the senior courts in Dublin.

For the I.R.A. the outcome of the battle confirmed for them that the policy and tactics of a guerrilla style campaign was the only way of doing battle with the Crown Forces. Conventional warfare had to be avoided at all costs. This included a guerrilla style skirmish developing into a conventional battle.

For the I.R.A. leadership at battalion level, the battle must have brought home to them their lack of formal military training and experience. This lack of experience was apparent not only prior to but at all stages of the battle. The outcome of the battle highlighted this deficiency. The fact that the commander had stayed at

Clonmult so long, the composition of the Reconnaissance Group, the fact that the sentries were prepared to leave their posts, and that the officer in command at the time allowed this, highlighted a lack of leadership, particularly in the heat of battle. There was no shortage of bravery but there was a lack of experienced leadership.

It was at a local level that the effects of the Battle of Clonmult were felt most. The battle was a devastating blow to the fighting efficiency of the 4th Battalion in Cork. The Battalion's Flying Column, effectively wiped out at Clonmult, had been its fighting echelon. The men who were killed and those that were captured had been the backbone of the column. There were others who were prepared to take their place but the weapons and ammunition so successfully captured during the skirmishes of 1920 could not be replaced. The R.I.C. barracks were now too well guarded and the British Army patrols had improved in both strength and vigilance.

For many years afterwards, Clonmult was the one battle most often spoken of by the surviving Cork veterans of the War of Independence. This was primarily because of the number of their comrades killed there; after all it was the I.R.A.'s greatest loss in a single battle. In time, however, the victories at Kilmichael, Crossbarry and other locations stole the limelight. It was sweeter to speak of battles won than of those lost.

The Battle of Clonmult

On the 20th day of February in 1921,
Our noble Midleton heroes
Were murdered in Clonmult,
For the fighting of their country's cause
To free her they did go,
But by an informer of our land,
In their grave they're lying low.

The bravest boys in Ireland,
That house they did command,
Brave Desmond Brothers stood there,
True rebels to the last,
And many another mother's son
With hearts full of grief did go,
To think that they should be betrayed
And their life's blood then left flow.
O'Hegarty you were a brave lad
And so was Ahern too,
Like the rest of the East Cork Martyrs
You were straight, firm and true,
Not forgetting Paddy Sullivan
And Moore as you now know
Who were executed in Cork Barracks,
And their life's blood then left flow.

'Twas on the Sabbath morning,
The district the 'Tans' did invade,
In search for Irish Rebels
Through many a hill and vale,
Surrounded were those boys at last
When rifle fire began,
And Desmond said–have courage lads
We have them nearly done

From the top of roof and window
Those lads went on to fight,
With the burning of the cottage
Left no escape in sight,
But still they kept on fighting
Till they fell one by one,
And the sad news left old Midleton
That the column boys were done.

God rest those brave young heroes
And in heaven may they find rest,
And the flag of freedom flying o'er
The Churchyards where they rest,
For this sacrifice our noble boys–
Tis plainly to be seen,
They said they'd fight and even die
For the Yellow, White and Green.

Clonmult's Lonely Vale

This story I will tell you, the truth I will unfold
About a group of volunteers who were betrayed for gold
Alas no more those lads we'll see, their loss we now bewail
They bravely died for Ireland's cause in Clonmult's Lonely Vale.

About a score of fighting men, this column did command
They came from East Cork and Athlone our freedom to demand
Their shelter was a farm house well off the beaten trail
Beyond Dungourney village in Clonmult's Lonely Vale.

On a fine spring day in February, the air was crisp and clear
When a Company of 'Black and Tans' and Hampshires did appear
A traitor's information had set them on the trail
To the peaceful little farmhouse in Clonmult's Lonely Vale.

It was a Sunday evening late in the afternoon
The Volunteers were breaking camp, they planned to march out soon
Two lads who went for water returned with an empty pail
When they heard the shout "surrender" in Clonmult's Lonely Vale.

This call was swiftly answered with a volley in reply
We stand for our Republic, we'll fight until we die
The Tans then set the roof ablaze while bullets flew like hail
And shot to death were twelve brave lads in Clonmult's Lonely Vale.

Now they lie in hallowed ground close by many a friend
Love of country was their crime, their land they did defend
No foe they feared those Volunteers, true sons of the Gael
A prayer recite for those who died in Clonmult's Lonely Vale.

Dick Cashman

In Memory of the Brave Boys
who Fell at Clonmult

In the glory of manhood and strength they came
To fight for their cause and true,
And the patriot fire in each breast aflame
Blazed brightly for Roisín Dhú.

Stout hearts full of hope on that threshold stood
Which led to the fields of death,
For the fury of foemen around them brewed
They felt it in every breath.

But never a shadow of fear knew they
It was theirs but to do or die,
Theirs to fall in the hush of a springtide day
'Neath the blue of an Irish sky.

They are gone, they're asleep in a martyr's grave
They have earned a martyr's crown,
Just one short year today their pure lives they gave
For love of Eire they laid them down.

But in letters of gold their names shall shine
Angels hover where oft' they've trod,
May they rest evermore in His realms divine
Those brave soldiers of Eire's sod.

(Mrs.) Isabel Burke,
Rocksavage, Cork.
20th of February, 1922.

APPENDICES

- I.R.A., order of battle, 1921, pertaining to Clonmult.

- Fourth Battalion Flying Column, members present at Clonmult.

- Nominal roll of the Fourth Battalion, Flying Column.

- British Army order of battle, 1921, pertaining to Clonmult

- Week-end casualties, 19th – 20th February, 1921

- Notice "B"

- British military communiqués, 20th and 22nd February, 1921

- R.I.C., monthly confidential report, February, 1921.

- Temporary County Inspector J.J.T. Carroll, R.I.C.

- Bravery medal awarded to Private Vautier for Clonmult

- Liut. A.R. Koe's Battle Report.

- Col. French's Letter of Commendation

- Field General v Drumhead court-martial

APPENDICES

Irish Republican Army
Order of Battle
1921

(Pertaining to Clonmult)

227

The members of the Flying Column killed at Clonmult were drawn primarily from 'A' and 'B' Companies, 4th Battalion, First Cork Brigade. Michael Leahy of Cobh was C.O. of the battalion.[228]

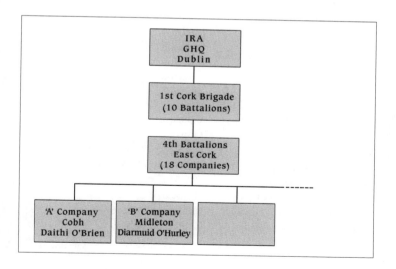

4th Battalion Flying Column Members present at Clonmult 20th of February 1921

Comdt. Diarmuid O'Hurley	Bandon
Vice-Comdt. Joseph Aherne	Midleton
Capt. James Ahern	Cobh
Capt. Richard Hegarty	Garryvoe
Capt. Paddy Higgins	Cloyne
Capt. Jack O'Connell	Cobh
Capt. Diarmuid O'Leary	Killeagh
Capt. Paddy Whelan	Wexford and Cobh
Lieut. Christopher O'Sullivan	Midleton
Lieut. Patrick O'Sullivan	Cobh
Vol. Jeremiah Aherne	Midleton
Vol. Liam Aherne	Midleton
Vol. Donal Dennehy	Midleton
Vol. David Desmond	Midleton
Vol. Michael Desmond	Midleton
Vol. James Glavin	Cobh
Vol. Michael Hallihan	Midleton
Vol. John Joe Joyce	Midleton
Vol. Maurice Moore	Cobh
Vol. Joseph Morrissey	Castlemartyr & Athlone
Na Fianna Vol. Jack Harty	Cloyne
Na Fianna Vol. William Garde	Shanagarry
Robert Walsh	Ballycotton
Edmund Terry	Churchtown South

Nominal Roll of the 4th Battalion Flying Column

Comdt. Diarmuid O'Hurley	Officer Commanding	Bandon
Vice-Comdt. Joseph Aherne	Second in Command	Midleton
Capt. Paddy Higgins	Quartermaster Officer	Cloyne
Capt. James Ahern	Cobh	
Capt. Richard Hegarty	Garryvoe	
Capt. Jack O'Connell	Cobh	
Capt. Diarmuid O'Leary	Killeagh	
Capt. Paddy Whelan	Wexford & Cobh	
Lieut. John Kelleher	Midleton	
Lieut. Christopher O'Sullivan	Midleton	
Lieut. Patrick O'Sullivan	Cobh	
Vol. Jack Aherne	Midleton	
Vol. Jeremiah Aherne	Midleton	
Vol. Liam Aherne	Midleton	
Vol. Tom Buckley	Midleton	
Vol. James Cagney	Midleton	
Vol. Daniel Cashman	Midleton	
Vol. Donal Dennehy	Midleton	
Vol. David Desmond	Midleton	
Vol. Michael Desmond	Midleton	
Vol. Joseph Duhig	Midleton	
Vol. James Glavin	Cobh	
Vol. Michael Hallihan	Midleton	
Vol. Jack Hyde	Ballinacurra	
Vol. Philip Hyde	Midleton	
Vol. Tom Hyde	Ballinacurra	
Vol. John Joe Joyce	Midleton	
Vol. Michael Kearney	Midleton	

Vol. Maurice Moore	Cobh
Vol. Joseph Morrissey	Castlemarty & Athlone
Vol. Michael Murnane	Midleton
Vol. Jim Mc Carthy	Midleton
Vol. David Stanton	Midleton
Vol. Patrick White	Midleton

British Army Order of Battle 1921

(Pertaining to Clonmult)

The British Army personnel involved in the Battle of Clonmult were drawn from the 2nd Battalion, Hampshire Regiment.[229]

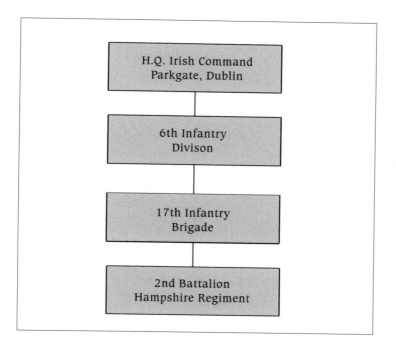

Week-end Casualties
19th – 20th February 1921

230

NOTICE "B"

WHEREAS ON the 17th day of May, 1921, cowardly and murderous attacks were carried out by armed rebels against the Forces of the Crown in the MIDLETON district,

and whereas there are good grounds for believing that you are a supporter of such rebels,

Now, therefore, I, COLONEL COMMANDANT, H.W. HIGGINSON, C.B., D.S.O. Commanding 17th Infantry Brigade and Military Governor, have ordered the destruction of your home.

Given under my hand at Cork this 17th day of May, 1921.

H.W. HIGGINSON
Colonel-Commandant
Military Governor

To:
THOMAS CASHMAN,
BALLINROSTIG.[231]

British military communiqués, 20th and 22nd February, 1921

Communiqué issued by Military General Headquarters on the night of Sunday 20th of February 1921:

This afternoon a party of the 2nd Battalion Hampshire Regiment surprised a party of armed civilians in a house near Midleton, Co. Cork (martial law area). The civilians split up, some taking up positions in the garden of the house, others firing from the house itself. After a fight of nearly two hours' duration, three wounded and five unwounded men were captured and thirteen were found dead.

A number of service rifles and a quantity of ammunition and bombs were also seized by the troops. One soldier was slightly wounded.[232]

Tuesday 22nd of February 1921
An official communiqué issued by General Headquarters, Parkgate states:

Further official details of the conflict which took place near Midleton, Co. Cork on Sunday, shows that a desperate defence was put up by the rebels who were eventually compelled to leave the open and take cover in the house.

Police reinforcements were quickly on the scene and the house was set on fire to drive out the defenders. Some came running out of the house, with their hands up, while others continued to fire on the Crown Forces as they went to accept the surrender.

The Commandant of the Midleton Company Irish Republican Army was amongst those killed. In addition to a large quantity of bombs, rifles and ammunition, a motor car was also captured.[233]

| **SECRET** | **County Inspector's Office** |
| **Crime Special** | **Cork 3-3-1921.** |

R.I.C., Monthly Confidential Report, February 1921

I beg to report that the state of the City and Riding is most unsatisfactory. Murders and attempts to murder are considerably on the increase, and many reports of ambushes in preparation for Crown Forces have been received. These outrages are attributable to the work of the Sinn Féin Organisation.

On Sunday 20th, Clonmult, a party of rebels in ambush were surprised by both police and military at Garrylawrence North of Midleton, in the Youghal District. Only one of the party succeeded in getting away – from information received this man was away at a farm house for supplies, the remaining 21 in number, were either, killed wounded or taken prisoner. The rebels first engaged a small party of Military from a house situated in an isolated position. The house had been put in a state of defence, and on the arrival of the police they were directing a heavy fire from it. They were dislodged by firing the roof and by bombing. They then tried to escape by a ruse. Some came from the building while those that remained inside opened fire on the police and military. The whole party was at once rushed and overcome. Fortunately the casualties to the Crown Forces were light, 1 soldier and 1 policeman being severely wounded and 1 officer and 2 police being slightly wounded. The rebels suffered 13 killed, 4 wounded, and 4 unwounded prisoners, of these 2 died subsequently. A large quantity of ammunition as well as service rifles, shot guns and revolvers were seized. The leader of the rebel gang – Jeremiah Hurley – who had been operating in this District for a considerable time is believed to have been killed in this attack, but the body was taken away during the night. It was the only body removed.

Signed: J.J.T. Carroll T.C.I.[234]

Temporary County Inspector J.J.T. Carroll,

Royal Irish Constabulary

Joseph J.T. Carroll, R.I.C. number 64531 was born in Dublin on the 28th of June, 1885. He was awarded a B.A. from the Royal University of Ireland. He received a commission during the First World War and served as a captain in the 6th Battalion, Royal Dublin Fusiliers from the 22nd of November, 1915 to the 24th of September, 1918, being twice wounded.

He was attached to the Crime Special Department, Dublin Castle from the 28th of September, 1918 to the 1st of May, 1920. His connection with the 4th Battalion Flying Column was that he was awarded the First Class favourable record for good duty in connection with an ambush at Ballyrichard (two miles west of Midleton on the Cork road) on the night of the 29th of December, 1920. The police under his command were on their way to Midleton following the attack by the 4th Battalion Column on an R.I.C. foot patrol on the Main Street when they were ambushed at Ballyrichard which is about two miles west of the town on the road to Cork. Three R.I.C. constables were killed in the two attacks two of whom were Black and Tans. It was the Columns last action prior to Clonmult. He lived in the Tivoli area of Cork. He married Miss Ethel Edith Coe on the 5th January 1922 and was pensioned out of the Force on the 8th of May, 1922.[235]

Bravery medal awarded to British soldier for Clonmult

Vautier, 5486823 Pte. C.G., 2nd Hampshires. Award of the medal was announced in the London Gazette on the 21st of April, 1921, (dated 1st of April, 1921).

The citation for the award stated: 'During an action on the 20th of February, 1921. Private Vautier held a one man sniper's post, in a very exposed position for over three hours being under all the time under intermittent fire at a range of from 20 to 30 yards, and succeeded in silencing the enemy fire and prevented them from forcing an entrance into the house which the Crown Forces were holding.'[236]

This incident, in which 12 I.R.A. men were killed, occurred at Clonmult, Co. Cork.

Medal presented in Dublin, 12th of July 1921.

Report of operations carried out by a party of the 2nd Bn HAMPSHIRE REGIMENT and a party of the R.I.C., on the 20th February, 1921

---

(1) A party of 2nd Bn Hampshire Regiment consisting of 4 Officers and 21 other ranks left Victoria Barracks at 14.15 hours 20. 2. 1921.

(2) The party arrived at RATHORGAN crossroads, about 5 miles south of T in, about 5 miles North of MIDLETON; at 15.00 hours.

(3) Leaving 1 N.C.O. and 6 O.R. in charge of the lorries, the remainder of the party proceeded across to a cottage 400 yards North of RATHORGAN crossroads.

(4) This cottage was searched without result. It was then decided to search a house, 400 yards N.E. of this cottage. This house is east of GARRYLAURENCE WOOD.

(5) The party moved there in two bodies. One consisting of Lieut's HAMMOND, M.C. and KOE and 7 O.R.s and the other of Lieut's HOOK, M.C. and DOVE and 6 O.R.s.

(6) Lieut. KOE and his party arrived near the house while the other party were 500 yards to the west of it. They arrived at approximately 15.45 hours.

(7) Fire was immediately opened on the leading party when they came near the house.

(8) Lieut. Koe and one man took cover in the lane EAST of the house. Four men of this party were lining the fence WEST of the house.

(9) Lieut. Hook M.C. and his party arrived at the fence west of the house at approximately 15.50 hours, and killed four men who were trying to escape.

(10) Lieut. Koe and one man joined Lieut. Hook M.C. at 16.05 hours.

(11) Three men were sent back to the lorries, which were ordered back to MIDLETON for bombs and reinforcements.

(12) Firing continued on both sides without result and it was feared that the result might be a stalemate owing to the inferior numbers of Crown Forces, but, reinforcements began to arrive under the County Inspector, Cork (South) who, himself, came on the scene at 17.20 hours. (Total reinforcements, 1 officer and 24 O.R.s.

(13) Lieut. Hammond, M.C. at 17.50 hours climbed over the fence north of the house and set alight the thatched roof of the house and directly afterwards bombs were thrown through the breach in the roof made by the fire. The R.I.C. suffered one casualty (severely wounded) during this period.

(14) At 18.20 hours the rebels signified that they wished to surrender and they were ordered to put up their hands and come out one by one. At 18.30 hours, six or seven rebels came out with their hands up and the Crown Forces went to meet them. On this fire was again opened by the remaining rebels in the house.

(15) Fire was at once re-opened on the house by the Crown Forces, and, in the cross fire which resulted, it was inevitable that casualties should be inflicted on the rebels outside the house by both sides. The Crown Forces, having re-opened fire, rushed to the house. When the house was captured, there were eight men in it, four wounded and four un-wounded. These were taken prisoner.

(16) C.S.M. CORNEY who was with Lieut. Koe was wounded when the rebels first opened fire. He was sent back to the lorries and while he was on his way to them, he was threatened with a bomb by a man who had escaped from the house during the first 5 minutes and who had already attempted to shoot Lieut. Hammond but had missed him at point blank range. C.S.M. Corney got away from this man, who was shot by one of the party guarding the lorries when he was actually trying to throw the bomb.

This man by his description is believed to be the man "JER. HURLEY", the captain of the MIDLETON Active Service COY., I.R.A. and is known to have been the leader of all I.R.A. activity in this area for some months.

(17) All arms and ammunition etc. were collected, but the numbers have not yet been ascertained definitely. They amount to about 10 – 15 rifles, some shot guns, and between 6 and 10 revolvers and automatics.

(18) The Crown Forces returned to Barracks arriving back at 21.00 hours.

Cork,   (Sgd) A.R. KOE, Lieut.
21.21.21. 2nd Bn. The Hampshire Regiment.

Col. French's Letter of Commendation

Headquarters
17th Infantry Brigade.

I forward herewith Lieut. Koe's report on operations carried out near Clonmult on 20.2.21. I allowed these operations to be carried out by the troops in the Cork area in order to save time and because the information on which they were based was obtained in Cork

I consider that the operation was well conceived and troops skilfully led and that the whole affair reflects the highest credit on both officers and men engaged.

I have much pleasure in bringing to your notice the names of Lieut. A.R. Koe and Lieut. Hammond M.C. The former of these officers was responsible for initiating and planning the operation and I should be glad if his name might be forwarded for a suitable decoration, and if possible the Military Cross. Apart from this affair he has done consistently good work.

Lieut. Hammond's action in setting light to the thatched roof of the house was an exceedingly gallant one which was largely responsible for the final result being achieved with so few casualties. I hope his name may be forwarded for suitable decoration. If possible, a bar to his Military Cross.

I have already forwarded Lieut. Hook's name for a decoration in connection with another affair and merely draw your attention to the fact that he was present on this occasion also and led his party skilfully.

In conclusion I consider it essential that on such occasions Officers would always carry rifles and that there should be a Very pistol with every lorry load of troops as a Very Light would probably set light to a thatched roof and in any case would be an unpleasant projectile to fire into a house. Stick Rifle Grenades would also be most useful in this sort of fighting.

I trust that the D.C. Cork may be informed that the support of the R.I.C. was timely, loyal and decisive and their ready and skilful co-operation was greatly appreciated both by the Officers and Troops concerned and also all ranks of this battalion.

Cork
21.2.21   (Sgd) C French
Colonel.
Commanding 2nd Bn Hampshire Regiment.

Field General v Drumhead court-martial

The early courts-martial in the martial law area were Field General Courts-Martial. This type of court-martial involved a civilian legal team defending the I.R.A. prisoners, a jury of three British Army officers, a legal prosecutor for the Crown and a senior British Army legal officer, acting as Judge-Advocate.

The Field General Court-Martial proceedings for the first Clonmult trial did not begin until fifteen days after the battle. The court-martial was spread out over twelve days even though it was not heard on all of these days. The end of the trial to the appeals in Dublin spanned thirty-one days and the appeal process took a further eight days to complete. At the end of these sixty-six days, two of the seven I.R.A. men were executed. The length of time involved was why General Strickland preferred to try the captured I.R.A. men by Drumhead Court-Martial.

All of the individuals officiating at a Drumhead Court-Martial were British Army officers. The I.R.A. prisoner was defended by a British officer, the jurors were British Army officers and the Judge-Advocate was a senior army officer. The first occasion that a captured I.R.A. prisoner was tried by Drumhead Court-Martial in the martial law area, was on Monday, 2nd of May, 1921. The day before, Sunday, a Crown Forces mobile patrol was ambushed near Kildorrery, in north Cork at approximately 5.30 p.m. The patrol overwhelmed the ambush party and in the ensuing battle two I.R.A. men were killed. Volunteer Patrick Casey was spotted by two soldiers firing his rifle. After firing a round at the same two soldiers, the I.R.A. man dropped his rifle and surrendered. He was taken to Victoria Barracks where he was tried by Drumhead Court-Martial the following day, he was found guilty and sentenced to death. He was executed at 6.00 p.m., that evening. The entire process from capture to execution took twenty-five hours. However, I.R.A. legal representatives appealed against this form of trial to the High Court in Dublin. The Attorney-General ruled that death sentences handed down following these trials must be confirmed by a superior court, before being carried out.

Bibliography

Unpublished Works

Ashe, B. *The Development of the I.R.A.'s Concepts of Guerrilla Warfare, 1917-1921*, M.A. Thesis, (U.C.C., 1996). Ref. DM 6328.

Borgonovo, J.M., *Informers, Intelligence and the "Anti-Sinn Féin Society", The Anglo-Irish Conflict in Cork City, 1920-1921*, M.A. Thesis, (U.C.C., 1997). Ref. DM 5930.

Girvin, K. E., *The Life and Times of Sean O'Hegarty, (1881-1963), O/C First Cork Brigade, War of Independence*, M. Phil. Thesis, (U.C.C., 2003). Ref. DM 7842.

Joy, S. M., *Co. Kerry, 1916-1921: A Provincial View of the I.R.A. and The War of Independence*, M. Phil. Thesis, (U.C.C., 2000). Ref. DM 6796.

O'Donoghue papers, National Library of Ireland.

Bureau of Military History, 1913–21, Individual Statements

Ahern, Eamonn, document number 39

Aherne, Joseph, document number 1367

Burke, Michael J., document number 1424

Cashman, Daniel, document number 1523

Fitzgerald, Seamus, document number 1737

Higgins, Patrick J., document number 1467

Hourihane, Thomas, document number 1366

Kearney, Comdt. Michael, document number 1418

Kelleher, John, document number 1456

Leahy, Michael, document number 94

O'Connell, Lieut. Col. John P., document number 1444

O'Leary, Diarmuid, document number 1589

Whelan, Comdt. Patrick J., document number 1449

Published Works

Abbott, Richard, *Police Casualties in Ireland, 1919-1922,* Mercier Press, Cork, 2000, ISBN 1 85635 314 1.

Barry, Tom, *Guerrilla Days in Ireland,* Irish Press Ltd., Dublin, 1949.

Barton, Brian, *From Behind a Closed Door, Secret Court Martial Records of the 1916 Easter Rising,* Blackstaff Press, Belfast, 2002, ISBN 0 85640 697 X.

Bennett, R., *The Black and Tans,* E. Hulton & Co. Ltd., London, 1959.

Breen, Dan, *My Fight for Irish Freedom,* Anvil Press, Tralee, 1975

Brennan-Whitmore W.J., *With the Irish in Frongoch,* The Talbot Press, Dublin, 1917.

Falvey, Jeremiah, *The Chronicles of Midleton 1700-1990,* Sira Publications, Cloyne, Co. Cork, 1998, ISBN 0 9534650 0 4.

Feeneey, P. J., *Glory O, Glory O, Ye Bold Fenian Men,* Dripsey, Co. Cork, 1996.

Fitzgerald, Seamus, East Cork Activities-1920, *The Capuchin Annual, 1970,* pp. 360-368.

Hanley, Brian, *A Guide to Irish Military Heritage,* Four Courts Press, Maynooth Research Guides for Irish Local History: Number 7, 2004, ISBN 1 85182 788 9, hardback, 1 85182 789 7, paperback.

Hart, Peter, *The I.R.A. and its Enemies, Violence and Community in Cork, 1916-1923,*

Oxford University Press, 1998, ISBN 0-19-820537-6.

Hart, Peter, *The I.R.A. at War 1916-1923,* Oxford University Press, 2003, ISBN 0 19 925258 0.

Hart, Peter, (ed.) *British Intelligence in Ireland, 1920-21, The Final Reports,* Cork University Press, 2002, ISBN 1 85918 201 1, pp 91 and 104n.

Harvey, D. and White, G., *The Barracks, A History of Victoria / Collins Barracks, Cork,* Mercier Press, Cork, 1997, ISBN 1 85635 194 7.

Hogan, David, (pseudo. Frank Gallagher), *The Four Glorious Years,* Irish Press Ltd., Dublin, 1953.

Hopkinson, Michael, *The Irish War of Independence,* Gill and Macmillan, Dublin, 2002, ISBN 0 7171 3010 X.

Macardle, Dorothy, *The Irish Republic,* Irish Press Ltd, Dublin, 1951.

Mac Eoin, Uinseann, *Survivors,* Argenta Publications, Dublin, 1980,

Mc Cann, John, Thirty Pieces of Silver, in, *War by the Irish,* The Kerryman, Tralee, 1946.

Mc Carthy, Kieran/Christensen, Maj-Britt, *Cobh's Contribution to the Fight for Irish Freedom, 1913 – 1990,* Oileann Mór Publications, Cobh, Co. Cork, 1992.

Maxwell, Henry, T., *The Irish Reports, 1921, Vol. 2, The King's Bench Division,*
The Incorporated Council of Law Reporting for Ireland, Dublin, 1921.

Monthly [British] Army List 1921, A distribution List of Officers on the Active List
of the Regular Army, the Royal Marines, H.M. Stationary Office, London.

Moore, Tony, *Clonmult and the Construction of a Legend,* A Dissertation for
Consideration by the University of Humberside as part of the B.A.
(Honours) Degree in Combined Studies, 1996.

National Graves Association, *The Last Post, Details and Stories of Irish
Republican Dead, 1916-1985,* Elo Press, Dublin, 1985.

O'Callaghan, Sean, *Execution,* Frederick Muller Limited, London, 1974.

O'Ciosain, Padraig, Operations in East Cork, *Rebel Corks Fighting Story
from 1916 to the Truce with Britain,* Anvil Press 1947.

O'Donoghue, Florence, *No Other Law,* Irish Press Ltd., Dublin, 1954.

O'Donoghue, Florence, *Tomás Mac Curtain,* The Kerryman Ltd., Tralee, 1958.

O'Farrell, Padraic, *Who's Who in the Irish War of Independence 1916-1921,* The
Mercier Press, Dublin and Cork, 1980, ISBN 0 85342 604 6.

O'Mahony, Sean, *Frongoch, University of Revolution,* FDR Teoranta, Dublin, 1987.

O'Riordán, Tomás, *The Price of Freedom,* Litho Printed, Barry's, Fermoy. n.d.

O'Toole, E.H., *Decorations and Medals of the Republic of Ireland,* (Medallic
Publishing Company, Connecticut, 1990), ISBN 0 9624663 5.

Rebel Cork's Fighting Story, from 1916 to the Truce with Britain, Kerryman edition, n.d.

Rebel Cork's Fighting Story, from 1916 to the Truce with Britain, Anvil Edition,
The Kerryman, Tralee, n.d.

Scott-Daniell, David, *The Regimental History of the Royal Hampshire
Regiment,* Gale and Polden, Aldershot, 1955, Vol. 3, 1918-1954.

Sheehan, Tim, *Execute Hostage Compton-Smith,* Dripsey Press, Co. Cork, 1993.

Sheehan, Tim, *Lady Hostage,* Dripsey Press, Co. Cork, 1990.

Townshend, Charles, *The British Campaign in Ireland 1919-1921, The
Development of Political and Military Policies,* Oxford University Press, 1975.

Twohig, Canon Patrick J., *Green Tears for Hecuba,* Tower Books,
Ballincollig, Co. Cork, 1994, ISBN 0 902568 23 X

White, G., and O'Shea, B., *The Irish Volunteer Soldier 1913 – 23,* Osprey
Publishing, Warrior Series No. 80, Wellingborough, Northants, U.K.,
2003, ISBN 1 84176 685 2.

White, G., and O'Shea, B., *Baptised in Blood, the formation of the Cork
Brigade of the Irish Volunteers 1913-1916,* Mercier Press, Cork, 2005,
ISBN 1 85635 465 2.

*With the I.R.A. in the Fight for Freedom 1919 to the Truce, the Red Path of
Glory,* Kerryman, Tralee, n.d.

Primary Sources and Interviews

Bureau of Military History, 1913-1921,

Statement by Witness

Aherne, Joseph,	Document No. 1367
Burke, Michael J,	Document No. 1424
Cashman, Daniel,	Document No. 1523
Fitzgerald, Seamus,	Document No. 1737
Higgins, Patrick J.,	Document No. 1467
Kelleher, John,	Document No. 1456
Leahy, Michael,	Document No. 94
O' Connell, John P,	Document No. 1444
O' Leary, Diarmuid,	Document No. 1589
Whelan, Patrick, J.	Document No. 1449

Interviews
Mrs. Theresa Cotter, Local (Carrigtwohill) historian.
Mr. James Hegarty witnessed the battle, audio taped interview with me,
7th December 2003 and 3rd March 2004.

Sources
C.A.I.	Cork Archives Institute
C.O.	Colonial Office
C.P.M.	Cork Public Museum
Mil. Arch.	Military Archives (Irish)
N.A.	National Archives, (U.K)
N.L.I.	National Library of Ireland
P.R.O.L.	Public Records Office, London
U.C.D., A.D.	U.C.D., Archive Department
W. S.	Witness Statement

Notes

1 Florence O'Donoghue, *Tomás MacCurtain,* (Irish Press Ltd., 1954), p.14.

2 Ibid. p.20.

3 Lieut. Col. Jack O'Connell, *Witness Statement No. 1367,* (Irish Military Archives, Cathal Brugha Barracks, Dublin), p.1.

4 Michael Leahy, *Witness Statement No.94,* (Irish Military Archives, Cathal Brugha Barracks), p.1.

5 Sean O'Mahony, *Frongoch, University of Revolution*, (F.D.R. Teoranta, 1987).

6 Ibid.

7 Ibid, p.172.

8 Michael Hopkinson, *The War of Independence,* (Gill and Macmillan, 2002), p.13.

9 David Hogan, (pseudo. Frank Gallagher), *The Four Glorious Years,* (Irish Press Ltd., Dublin, 1953).

10 John Kelleher, *Witness Statement No.1456,* (Irish Military Archives, Dublin), p.1.

11 Paddy Higgins, *Witness Statement No.1467,* (Irish Military Archives), p.2.

12 Joseph Aherne, *Witness Statement No.1367,* (Irish Military Archives), p.2.

13 Ibid. p.2.

14 Tomás O'Riordán, 'Diarmuid O'Hurley', in, *Imokilly People Newspaper,* 7th June, 2001, p.15.

15 Patrick Whelan, *Witness Statement No.1449,* (Irish Military Archives), p.1.

16 Joseph Aherne, *Witness Statement No 1367,* p.1.

17 Florence O'Donoghue, *Tomas MacCurtain,* p.151.

18 Ibid.

19 Seamus Fitzgerald, 'East Cork Activities-1920', in, *The Capuchin Annual 1970,* Dublin, p.360.

20 Kieran McCarthy and Maj-Britt Christensen, *Cobh's Contribution to the Fight for Irish Freedom 1913-1990,* (Oileánn Mór Publications, Cobh, 1992), pp.28-34.

21 David Hogan, *The Four Glorious Years,* p.55.

22 Charles Townshend, *The British Campaign in Ireland, 1919-1921, The Development of Political and Military Policies,* (Oxford University Press, 1975), p.15.

23 Ibid. p.15.

24 Dorothy Macardle, *The Irish Republic,* (Irish Press Ltd., Dublin, 1951), p.274.

25 Dan Breen, *My Fight for Irish Freedom,* (Anvil Books, Tralee, 1975), pp.38-58, also, Richard Abbott, *Police Casualties in Ireland 1919–1922,* (Mercier Press, Cork, 2000), pp.30-33.

26 *Rebel Corks Fighting Story,* (Anvil Book, Tralee, n.d.), pp 179-189.

27 Patrick Whelan, *Witness Statement No. 1449,* p.29.

28 Padraig O'Farrell, *Who's Who in the Irish War of Independence,* (Mercier Press, Cork, 1980), p.128.

29 U.C.D., A.D., *O'Malley Papers,* p.17 b/114.

30 Paddy Whelan, *Witness Statement No. 1449,* pp.35 & 36.

31 Ibid., p.37.

32 U.C.D., A.D., *Organisational Memo No. 1,* p.17b/127.

33 Paddy Whelan, *Witness Statement No. 1449,* p.38.

34 *Rebel Corks Fighting Story,* pp.187 & 188.

35 Richard Abbott, *Police Casualties in Ireland 1919–1922,* pp.168 & 169.

36 Joseph Aherne, *Witness Statement No.1367,* p.55.

37 Ibid.

38 Richard Abbott, *Police Casualties in Ireland 1919–1922,* p.169.

39 Ibid.

40 Tomás O'Riordán, east Cork historian.

41 Jack O'Connell, Witness Statement No. 1444, p.8. Also, Joseph Aherne, Witness Statement No. 1367, p.51.

42 Tom Barry, *Guerrilla Days in Ireland,* (Irish Press, Dublin), p.19.

43 Ibid.

44 *Ordnance Survey Maps*, 1904, Sheet No. 54, Munster, Cork, Boole Library, U.C.C.

45 Ibid.

46 Joseph Aherne, *Witness Statement No. 1367,* p.54.

47 Seamus Fitzgerald, Witness *Statement No. 1737,* p.34.

48 Jack O'Connell, *Witness Statement No. 1444,* p.14.

49 Ibid.

50 Patrick Whelan, Witness *Statement No. 1449,* p.52.

51 Jack O'Connell, *Witness Statement No. 1444,* p.8.

52 C.A.I., John Hallinan's photograph album.

53 Ibid.

54 Joseph Aherne, *Witness Statement No. 1367,* p.52.

55 Ibid. p.55.

56 Patrick Whelan, *Witness Statement No. 1449,* p.50.

57 Joseph Aherne, *Witness Statement No. 1367,* p.51.

58 British in Ireland, Reel No. 74, Jan–March 1921, *R.I.C. County Inspector's Monthly Confidential Report, February 1921,* CO 904/114, Boole Library, U.C.C.

59 Jack O'Connell, *Witness Statement No. 1444,* p.13.

60 Extract from a letter written by a sister of Dick Hegarty, Hegarty family archives.

61 Letter in Hegarty family archives.

62 *Cork Examiner,* Wednesday, 15th March, 1921.

63 Patrick Whelan, *Witness Statement No. 1449,* p.52.

64 Joseph Aherne, *Witness Statement No. 1367,* p.51 and Patrick Whelan, *Witness Statement* No. 1449, p.50.

65 Patrick Whelan, *Witness Statement No. 1449,* p.51.

66 Patrick Whelan, *Witness Statement No. 1449,* p.52.

67 Ibid. p.52

68 Joseph Aherne, *Witness Statement No. 1367,* p.55.

69 Ibid.

70 *Rebel Corks Fighting Story*, p.191 see also, John Mc Cann, 'Thirty Pieces of Silver', in, *War by the Irish,* (The Kerryman, Tralee, 1946), p.153.

71 David Scott-Daniell, *The Regimental History of the Royal Hampshire Regiment,* (Gale and Polden, Aldershot, 1955), Vol. 3, p.10.

72 Michael Hennessy, in, Tony Moore's, *Clonmult and the Construction of Legend*, (University of Humberside, B.A. Thesis, 1996), p.11.

73 N.L.I., *O'Donoghue Papers*, MS 31223 (1).

74 *Regimental History of the Royal Hampshire Regiment,* Vol. 3. pp 9 – 11.

75 *Lieut. A.R. Koe's after action report,* see appendix 11

76 *Cork Examiner,* Wednesday, 16th March 1921.

77 Diarmuid O'Leary, *Witness Statement, No. 1589,* (Irish Military Archives), p.5.

78 *Cork Examiner,* Wednesday, 9th March, 1921.

79 Lochlinn McGlynn and Ray Ryan, *The Kerryman,* Saturday 20th February, 1965, p.9.

80 Jack O'Connell, *Witness Statement No. 1444,* p.14.

81 Ibid. p.10.

82 Ibid.

83 Jack O'Connell, *Witness Statement No. 1444,* p.14.

84 Tony Moore, *Clonmult and the Construction of a Legend*, p.15, also, *Lieut. Koe's report.*

85 Diarmuid O'Leary, *Witness Statement No. 1589,* p.6.

86 Ibid. p. 7.

87 Diarmuid O'Leary, *Witness Statement No. 1589,* p.7.

88 Jim Herlihy, Gárda and R.I.C. historian to author.

89 Michael Hopkinson, *The Irish War of Independence,* p.92.

90 Ibid. p.93.

91 Paddy Higgins, *Witness Statement No. 1467,* p.7.

92 *Cork Examiner,* Unnamed British Army officer's evidence, 9th March, 1921.

93 *Cork Examiner*, Wednesday, 14th March, 1921.

94 Joseph Aherne, *Witness Statement No. 1367*, p.57.

95 Patrick Higgins, *Witness Statement*, p.6, also, Diarmuid O'Leary, *Witness Statement No. 1589*, p.7.

96 *Rebel Corks Fighting Story*, p.195, also, Diarmuid O'Leary, *Witness Statement No. 1589*, p.7.

97 Not 13 dead as reported in the newspapers.

98 British in Ireland, Reel No. 74, Jan–March 1921, *R.I.C. County Inspector's Monthly Confidential Report, February 1921*, CO 904/114.

99 Ibid.

100 Tony Moore, *Clonmult and the Creation of a Legend*, p.18.

101 Jack O'Connell, *Witness Statement No. 1444*, p.10.

102 Jim Hegarty, *Interview with author.*

103 Jack O'Connell, *Witness Statement No. 1444*, p.11.

104 Jim Hegarty, *Interview with author.*

105 Jack O'Connell, *Witness Statement No. 1444*, p.11.

106 Ibid.

107 Jim Hegarty, *Interview with author.*

108 Jack O'Connell, *Witness Statement No. 1444*, p.15.

109 See map, p.66.

110 Ibid.

111 Patrick Whelan, *Witness Statement No. 1449*, p.53.

112 M. J. Corry, 1889–1979, Fianna Fail T.D. for east Cork 1927–1969.

113 Joseph Aherne, *Witness Statement No. 1367*, p.52.

114 Ibid.

115 Patrick Whelan, *Witness Statement No. 1449*, p.54.

116 Jim Hegarty, *Interview with author.*

117 Joseph Aherne, *Witness Statement No. 1367*, p.53.

118 Patrick Whelan, *Witness Statement No. 1449*, p.54.

119 Ibid.

120 Daniel Cashman, *Witness Statement No. 1523*, (Irish Military Archives), p.10.

121 Patrick Higgins, *Witness Statement No. 1467*, p.6.

122 Jack O'Connell, *Witness Statement No. 1444,* p.8.

123 *Military Communiqué,* (British Army Headquarters, Dublin), 22nd February 1921.

124 Unnamed British Army Officer, *Cork Examiner,* Wednesday, 15th March, 1921.

125 *Cork Examiner,* Monday, 21st February, 1921.

126 British in Ireland, Reel No. 74, Jan-March 1921, *R.I.C. County Inspector's Monthly Confidential Report, February, 1921.* CO 904/114.

127 Jeremiah Falvey, *The Chronicles of Midleton 1700-1990,* (Sira Publications, Cloyne, 1990) p.146.

128 Ibid.

129 Kieran McCarthy and Maj-Britt Christensen, *Cobh's Contribution to the Fight for Irish Freedom 1913-1990,* p.82.

130 Jeremiah Falvey, *The Chronicles of Midleton,* p.146.

131 Ibid.

132 Later, Canon Francis Flannery, Castlemartyr.

133 Joseph Aherne, *Witness Statement No. 1367,* p.53.

134 Diarmuid O'Leary, *Witness Statement No. 1589,* pp.8 – 9.

135 British in Ireland, Reel No. 74, Jan-March 1921, *R.I.C. County Inspector's Monthly Confidential Report, February 1921.* CO 904/114.

136 *Irish Times,* Wednesday, 9th March, 1921.

137 Brian Barton, *From Behind a Closed Door, Secret Court Martial Records of the 1916 Easter Rising,* (Blackstaff Press, Belfast, 2002), p.20.

138 Ibid. p.28.

139 *Cork Examiner,* Wednesday, 9th March, 1921.

140 *Irish Times,* Wednesday, 9th March, 1921.

141 *Cork Examiner,* Wednesday, 9th March, 1921.

142 Ibid.

143 *Cork Examiner,* Wednesday, 14th March, 1921.

144 Ibid.

145 *Cork Examiner,* Wednesday, 15th March, 1921.

146 Ibid.

147 Ibid.

148 Ibid.

149 *Cork Examiner,* Wednesday, 16th March, 1921.

150 Ibid.

151 Ibid.

152 *Cork Examiner,* Wednesday, 17th March, 1921.

153 Ibid.

154 *Cork Examiner,* Wednesday, 19th March, 1921.

155 Ibid.

156 T. Henry Maxwell, *The Irish Reports, 1921, Vol. 2, The King's Bench Division,* The Incorporated Council of Law Reporting for Ireland, Dublin, 1921, p.317.

157 Ibid.

158 *The Irish Reports, 1921, Vol. 2, The King's Bench Division,* pp.319 and 320.

159 Ibid. p.329.

160 Ibid. p.325.

161 Ibid. p.327.

162 Ibid. pp.328 and 329.

163 Ibid. p.332.

164 *Cork Examiner,* Wednesday, 27th April, 1921.

165 P.J. Feeney, *Glory O, Glory O, Ye Bold Fenian Men,* (Dripsey, Co. Cork, 1996), p.156.

166 Florence O'Donoghue, *No Other Law,* pp.137 & 138.

167 Tom Barry, *Guerrilla Days in Ireland,* p.93.

168 P.J. Feeney, *Glory O, Glory O, Ye Bold Fenian Men,* p.156.

169 Sean O'Callaghan, *Execution,* (Fredrick Muller Ltd., London, 1974), p.144.

170 Ibid. p.161.

171 Tim Sheehan, *Execute Hostage Compton-Smith,* (Dripsey Press, 1993) p.79.

172 P.J. Feeney, *Glory O, Glory O, Ye Bold Fenian Men,* p.157.

173 Tim Sheehan, *Execute Hostage Compton-Smith,* p.86.

174 *Rebel Cork's Fighting Story,* p.195.

175 *Rebel Corks Fighting Story,* (Kerryman edition only), p.157 also, *Cork Examiner,* 6th May, 1921.

176 Diarmuid O'Leary, *Witness Statement No. 1589,* p.11.

177 Canon O'Sullivan was diocesan administrator and Father O'Brien was the prison chaplain and also curate in the North Cathedral, see Sean O'Callaghan, *Execution,* pp.153 and 154.

178 *Cork Examiner,* 29th April, 1921.

179 Ibid.

180 Diarmuid O'Leary, *Witness Statement No. 1589,* p.11.

181 *Cork Examiner,* 30th April, 1921.

182 Tim Sheehan, *Execute Hostage Compton-Smith,* pp.107–109.

183 Ibid.p.108.

184 Ibid.p.110.

185 Tim Sheehan, *Execute Hostage Compton-Smith,* pp.110.

186 *CI Monthly Report,* East Cork May 1921, (CO 904/115), see also, *Rebel Cork's Fighting Story,* p.197, also Peter Hart, *The I.R.A. & Its Enemies, Violence and Community in Cork, 1916-1923,* (Oxford University Press, 2002), p.98.

187 52111, Gunner Michael O'Keeffe served in the Royal Artillery during the First World War, he is buried in the old graveyard in Carrigtwohill.

188 Peter Hart, *The I.R.A. & Its Enemies,* p.98.

189 Richard Abbott, *Police Casualties in Ireland 1919-1922,* p.227.

190 *Cork Examiner,* 9th May, 1921.

191 *Cork Examiner,* 10th May, 1921.

192 Richard Abbott, *Police Casualties in Ireland 1919-1922,* p.238.

193 *Cork Examiner,* 16th May, 1921.

194 Ibid.

195 *Rebel Cork's Fighting Story,* p.197.

196 *Cork Examiner,* 16th & 17th May, 1921.

197 N.L.I., *O'Donoghue papers,* MS 31,207 (2).

198 P.R.O. London, CO 904/168, also, B. Ashe, *The Development of the I.R.A.'s Concepts of Guerrilla Warfare, 1917-1921,* (U.C.C., 1996), also, N.L.I., *O'Donoghue Papers,* MS 31,207 (2).

199 NLI, *O'Donoghue papers,* MS 31,207 (2).

200 Glenville was designated as 'C' Company, 1st Battalion, 2nd Brigade, I.R.A.

201 Peter Hart, editor, *British Intelligence in Ireland 1920-21, The Final Reports,* 'Irish Narratives' (Cork University Press, 2002), p.91.

202 Ibid.

203 Jack O'Connell, *Witness Statement No. 1444,* pp.18 and 19.

204 *Rebel Cork's Fighting Story,* p.197.

205 R. Henchion, *Journal of the Cork Historical and Archaeological Society,* Vol. LXXVIII, No. 227, Jan.-Jun. 1973, pp.49–51.

206 Patrick Whelan, *Witness Statement No. 1449,* p.56.

207 *Regimental History of the Royal Hampshire Regiment,* Vol. 3, p.11.

208 Patrick J. Twohig, *Green Tears for Hecuba,* (Tower Books, Ballincollig, Co. Cork, 1994), pp.337–344, also, Sean O'Callaghan, *Execution,* pp.181 and 182, also pp.189–192.

209 Patrick Higgins, *Witness Statement No. 1467,* p.4.

210 *Cork Examiner,* Tuesday, 28th June, 1921.

211 Ibid. Wednesday, 22nd June, 1921.

212 Ibid. Tuesday, 28th June, 1921.

213 Ibid. 22nd June, 1921.

214 Ibid.

215 Ibid.

216 Ibid.

217 Patrick Higgins, *Witness Statement No. 1467,* p.7.

218 *Cork Examiner,* Tuesday, 28th June, 1921.

219 Ibid.

220 Ibid. Wednesday, 20th July, 1921.

221 Ibid.

222 Ibid. Friday, 8th July, 1921.

223 Ibid. Friday, 15th July, 1921.

224 *Capuchin Annual, 1970,* p.360.

225 Ibid.

226 Townshend, *The British Campaign in Ireland 1919-1921,* pp.53 and 144.

227 *Freeman's Journal,* Monday, 21st February, 1921.

228 Cashman family artefacts.

229 *Freeman's Journal,* Monday 21st Feb., 1921.

230 Ibid.

231 British in Ireland, Reel No. 74, Jan–March 1921, *R.I.C. County Inspector's Monthly Confidential Report, February 1921.* CO 904/114

232 The Church of Jesus Christ of Latter Day Saints, micro film, ref. LDF 0852098/224 received from Gárda Jim Herlihey.

233 M.D. Cassell, 'Awards of the Medal of the Order of the British Empire for Gallantry in Ireland, 1920 to 1922', in, *The Journal of the Orders and Medals Research Society (U.K.)* Vol. No.25, Winter 1986, No.4, (193), p.213.

Index